MANAGING ANGER

Helen O'Neill, MSc, DipCOT, SROT
Senior Occupational Therapist
St Andrew's Hospital, Northampton

Illustrations by Clive Kemp

Whurr Publishers Ltd

© 1999 Whurr Publishers
First published 1999 by
Whurr Publishers Ltd
19b Compton Terrace, London N1 2UN, England

Reprinted 2000 (twice), 2001 (twice) and 2002

British Library Cataloguing in Publication Data
A catalogue record for this book is available from the
British Library.

ISBN: 1 86156 107 5

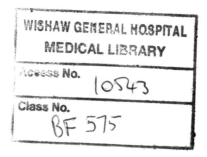
Printed and bound in the UK by Athenaeum Press Ltd,
Gateshead, Tyne & Wear

CONTENTS

ACKNOWLEDGEMENTS

I would like to thank all the colleagues and patients who have encouraged me to formalise my session plans and to produce this manual. A special thanks to 'Creative Clive' for the drawings and to Kirsty Pope (née Watkins), whose interest and user feedback was a driving force to me. She is also responsible for designing the signpost hand-out 'The assertive way'. This was created to illustrate an individual's choice of response and to clarify the meaning of some rather long words!

Throughout the manual I have tried to reference the original source of material but some of the practical ideas have evolved from session materials acquired over the years, and their origin is not always clear! Therefore I cannot claim originality for all diaries and worksheets and apologise to any who may feel that their ideas are being reprinted as my own.

Lastly, thanks to my family for their tolerance and willingness to share the computer!

THE PURPOSE OF THE MANUAL

This manual aims to provide a series of session plans to help the therapist lead a course of anger management treatment with individuals who have cognitive impairment. 'The term cognitive or intellectual impairment has been used to refer to any underlying loss or disturbance of basic psychological functions which may result in the person experiencing a learning disability' (World Health Organisation).

Why the manual was developed

The technique of managing problematic anger has become a widely used intervention in a variety of settings, including forensic, general mental health and non-clinical. A major contributor to this work for more than 20 years has been Professor Ray Novaco of the University of California. He has developed a model of anger, an anger scale (Novaco 1994a) and a stress inoculation procedure (Novaco 1993–4) for anger control. This is outlined on page 10.

The work of Novaco and that of Feindler and Ecton (1986), who refined the principles for use with adolescents, is suitable for individuals of average intellectual ability. However, therapists are frequently asked to treat individuals who have cognitive impairment. This request may present a difficulty for therapists; first, because it may be asked if a cognitive-behavioural treatment is appropriate for this population, and second, if it is, then how can it be applied?

Attention is now being given to answering these questions. A recent publication (Kroese, Dagnan and Loumidis 1997) describes the application of cognitive-behavioural treatment, including assessment and intervention, for individuals with learning disabilities. Black, Cullen and Novaco (1997) review what little research has been carried out using anger management procedures with this group and reveal some success.

So in practice, clinical experience has highlighted a need to adapt existing anger management treatment procedures to suit those clients with cognitive impairment. As a consequence, this treatment manual was developed for therapists dealing with such clients. It is based on the sound theoretical knowledge of Novaco, Meichenbaum and Feindler, but has looked towards additional influences, thus enabling the method of application to be adjusted to suit the needs of this population.

Recently, I have been working with individuals who have an acquired brain injury, and this has provided me with a challenge to tailor the delivery of treatment to suit this group also. Many such clients have problems with intense anger arousal that seemingly occurs instantly. They may, of course, have any number of possible deficits in the areas of attention, memory, problem-solving, perceptual or motor skills, and/or communication difficulties. Any of these may contribute to frustration and anger arousal, so it is important to be mindful of such difficulties when delivering treatment.

However, the greatest appreciation on my behalf, has been of the importance of environmental factors on information processing. This became obvious only as I listened to clients describe the acute distress of escalating physiological arousal and angry cognitions that accompany their attempt to make sense of a situation in a noisy or busy environment.

This fits comfortably with Novaco's perspective that 'anger can be a stress reaction activated by exposure to environmental elements and conditions that are categorised as stressors' (Novaco 1994b). A person in the midst of acute stress experiences a reduction in their ability to make sense of a situation as their attempts to process information may become chaotic or ineffective. Fortunately, in most cases the stress passes and the function resumes, but for those clients with acquired brain injury it is not just a temporary state.

Hence my recent work has provided me with a greater understanding of the process of anger arousal. At best the process is a complex one. As we analyse this process, to discover the sequence of events for the individual concerned, we realise that there are many opportunities for misinterpretations, misunderstandings and reactive responses. These can lead to the appraisal of anger in anybody, but if the individual involved has cognitive deficits or impairment, then surely there may be additional potential for the sequence to go wrong.

The development of this manual reflects both experience gained in clinical practice, including feedback from clients, and the influences of occupational therapy and psychology colleagues.

Note: The term 'cognitive impairment' has been defined, and will be used during the course of the manual. However, when studies are referred to, the terminology used in the particular study will be quoted; for example, learning disability, mental handicap, or developmentally and emotionally disabled.

MANUAL

THEORETICAL BACKGROUND

Anger is said to be the most talked about but least studied emotion (Novaco 1978). It would seem that anger affects the vast majority of people at times and that, when experienced, involves a combination of cognitive, physiological, behavioural and social components.

Yet, until recently, if it was studied, it was usually in conjunction with aggression or hostility rather than as an emotion in its own right. This may be because anger has no 'automatic status' as a clinical problem and does not have a formal classification in the Diagnostic and Statistical Manual of Mental Disorders IV (American Psychiatric Association 1994). It does, however, contribute to diagnoses such as post-traumatic stress disorder (PTSD) and borderline personality disorder, and is implicated in a number of clinical disorders (Novaco 1986).

Eckhardt and Deffenbacher (1995) belong to a body of professionals who believe that there is reason to research anger and give attention to the related social and medical problems affecting society. They assert that, like anxiety and depression, anger can also present in severe and extreme forms. The likelihood of it becoming a problem or dysfunctional increases with the intensity, frequency and duration of the anger, or when it leads to more frequent and severe consequences. Put another way, if the costs of the anger outweigh any activating benefits, it may well be a problem. Costs to the individual may be gradual, such as effects on physical health (McKay, Rogers and McKay 1989), or there may be immediate and obvious social costs following a direct behavioural response of angry aggression. This is probably the most frequent reason that a client is referred for anger management.

Definitions

The terms anger, aggression, hostility and violence are commonly used, yet there does not seem to be an absolute definition of any of them. This ambiguity is often referred to when reading the literature. Similarly, when talking to clients and some fellow professionals, it becomes clear that the terms are often clumped together in people's minds.

For the purpose of this manual the following definitions will be used.

Anger can be understood as a subjective emotional state defined by the presence of physiological arousal and cognitions of antagonism (Novaco 1994b). It is a normal emotion having many adaptive features, yet when the frequency, intensity or duration of anger outweigh its adaptive features, it is said to be dysfunctional (Novaco 1992).

Spielberger (1988) divided anger into two types, trait anger (the individual differences of disposition) and state anger (the temporary emotional state arising from frustration or annoyance of the moment). The division was an attempt to separate the personality factors peculiar to individuals, from the external factors that could anger any of us.

Aggression refers to overt behaviour, either physical or verbal, that does or could bring harm to another person, object or system (Eckhardt and Deffenbacher 1995). Barratt (1994) classifies aggression broadly into three categories: (1) premeditated or learned aggression, which varies between social groups and cultures; (2) medically related aggression, which may be secondary to illness, including psychopathology; and (3) impulsive aggression, which is characterised by a 'hair-trigger' temper. This is a helpful categorisation when considering the role of anger in aggression.

Hostility is a personality trait referring to appraisal and cognitive processes through which the individual tends to code others' actions as harmful and unjustified attacks (Eckhardt and Deffenbacher 1995). Hostility reflects a long-standing style of appraisal. It may evoke anger or a cold detachment, or prompt the planning and/or implementation of a vengeful act. This is in contrast to an isolated angry or aggressive response triggered by a specific provocation.

Violence comprises those acts in which there is a deliberate attempt to inflict physical harm; thus accidental harm does not comprise violence (Breakwell 1989).

There is considerable overlap between aggression and violence, the former often being used by psychologists and behavioural biologists, whereas someone with a legal background may use the term violence. Consequently, in the text of this manual the term aggression will be used.

What causes anger?

It is widely assumed that anger occurs as a result of frustration, perceived threat or a belief that a personal injustice has occurred. Common triggers are social or interpersonal in nature. They may be related to a direct external situation, such as being thwarted (*'he made me angry'*), or internal stimuli, such as memories and images when 'running old tapes'. Either of the above may then lead to brooding, ruminating or worry.

Anger may occur after anxiety, when an immediate fear is over but the annoyance of being put in the position of needing to worry, dawns on the person (*'why did they stay out so late, I thought they were hurt'*). All of this can be influenced by a person's pre-anger state, i.e. how tired, grumpy, hot, hungry and stressed they are. Novaco (1994b) sees anger as an effective stress reaction.

Does anger cause aggression?

There is considerable overlap between anger, hostility and aggression, yet one does not necessarily lead to the other. An angry person may or may not express their anger, and if they do, it can be in a variety of forms. Some may be aggressive towards other people or objects, but others may be adaptive, for example when using assertion.

Likewise, not all aggression is caused by anger (Howells 1989). Some aggression can be seen as instrumental. It is not fuelled by a strong emotional bias but by achieving a desired effect or goal, for example to intimidate or bully another person. This is different from angry, hostile aggression where behaviour is driven by anger and high levels of affect.

This distinction is very relevant in the case of managing problematic anger. A client presenting with instrumental aggression that has a 'pay-off' is unlikely to be motivated to change their behaviour. In contrast, a client who is overwhelmed by their escalating anger and 'hair-trigger' temper may show impulsive aggression, only to regret it later.

A model of anger

The Novaco model of anger was originally described by Novaco (1994a) but was also shown in O'Neill (1995). The model takes a contextual view of anger and places emphasis on environmental factors as well as internal processes.

> The basic conception is that anger is a subjective emotional state, entailing the presence of physiological arousal and cognitions of antagonism, and is a causal determinant of aggression. The 'subjective affect' element of anger is a cognitive labelling of the emotional state as angry or something semantically proximate, such as annoyed. This cognitive labelling is a highly automatic process, neither deliberate nor necessarily in tandem to the arousal. Associated with this cognitive labelling process is an inclination to act in an antagonistic or confrontational manner towards the source of the provocation. This action impulse is regulated by inhibitory mechanisms (internal and external controls) which may be overridden by disinhibitory influences (such as heightened arousal, aggressive modelling, low probability of punishment, biochemical agents, and contextual cues for aggression). Although provoking events are typically aversive (something the person would choose to avoid), people may engineer their own anger experiences by deliberate exposure to either external or internal stimuli; the arousal of anger may be satisfying as well as being functional.
>
> The relationship of anger to aggression is that it is a significant activator of and has a mutually influenced relationship with aggression, but it is neither necessary nor sufficient for aggression to occur (Novaco 1994a, pp. 32–33).

This forms a sound framework that underpins assessment and treatment interventions. The Novaco anger control is a cognitive-behavioural treatment based on the stress inoculation approach developed by Meichenbaum (1975, 1985). An outline of the training procedure follows.

OUTLINE OF THE STRESS INOCULATION TREATMENT FOR ANGER CONTROL

The treatment is a three-stage procedure and, although they are described sequentially, in practice they are interrelated within treatment sessions.

Cognitive preparation

This stage lays down the foundations of any changes that may be made throughout treatment. It includes assessment and interview, and is a time when the therapist and client begin to form a collaborative working relationship. The aim is to reach joint goals of treatment and establish a therapeutic alliance. During this stage, the individual is encouraged to develop an understanding of the components of his or her anger, how it differs from aggression and how the two are related. Training on emotional awareness and differential may be necessary because this is required before there can be a specific focus on anger.

The positive as well as the negative features of anger are discussed and a cost/benefit analysis carried out. It is pointed out that anger management is not about 'taking away the anger'; indeed, Novaco stresses that many individuals would be afraid of 'being robbed of their anger', feeling that it would also rob them of their ability to stop aversive situations. Instead, the training is meant to empower the individual, allowing him or her to become an expert in understanding and dealing with his or her own anger arousal.

The concept of self-monitoring is introduced as a necessary part of the treatment. The skill required for this technique may have to be taught to the client. A person's perception of his or her own anger and/or aggression is important, and may in turn relate to his or her motivation to change. If anger is seen to be a benefit rather than a cost, treatment interventions will be resisted. It is worth noting that these costs may not be the same to the individual concerned as they are to his or her family, spouse, fellow clients or the treatment team. If an individual clings to his or her anger, or if it pays dividends, he or she is unlikely to form a collaborative working relationship. Therefore, this stage involves client education and establishes the necessary therapeutic alliance.

Skill acquisition phase

This stage involves teaching cognitive-behavioural coping techniques that can be used when there is a sense of provocation. The individual is trained to see anger as a warning sign of which to take heed, and to decide upon which course of action to take; for example, he or she may ignore the provocation – 'there's no hope of winning' – and concentrate on reducing arousal levels or use assertion to express effectively a justified annoyance. As these coping skills become more effective, confidence levels increase. The individual has, therefore, a wider choice of response rather than simply resorting to anger and/or aggression. This is an important message to get across because it can promote compliance with this treatment.

In order to provide a structured way of implementing this, the process considers the three components of anger arousal (cognitive, arousal and behavioural) in turn. However, some of the techniques used, such as self-monitoring using cognitive-behavioural diaries or self-instruction, are applicable to each component.

1. The cognitive component

This part draws on the work of Beck and Ellis (cited in Novaco 1978). Treatment attempts to change overt behaviour by altering thoughts, interpretations, assumptions and strategies of responding.

Honest self-monitoring is required here, and by using diaries it is possible to gain access to the individual's 'hot cognitions'. This allows both the person concerned and the therapist to become aware of the following:

- the potential triggers on which the individual focuses (one can only get angry about something if one notices it in the first place), such as particular people, their habits, events, comments. Hence biases of attentional focus are identified.

- the individual's appraisal of a situation, including expectation of himself or herself and others
- thoughts that may fuel anger (wind-up thoughts).

The self-monitoring leads into identification of negative or wind-up thoughts. Thought-stopping techniques are used to arrest these wind-up thoughts and, at the same time, arousal reduction is implemented. Training modifies attentional focus and therefore provides a balance to the interpretation of an incident. As irrational thoughts and unrealistic expectations are identified, individuals are taught the techniques of cognitive restructuring, so they can challenge or moderate them.

The individual is trained to use self-instruction to direct himself or herself in a controlled way. Self-instruction statements can be used, for example:

(a)   when preparing for what may be a provoking situation: *remember, stick to the issues and don't take it personally*

(b)   when confronting and handling anger: *don't make more of this than you have to; you don't have to prove yourself*

(c)   when reducing levels of arousal: *my muscles are getting tight, time to relax*

(d)   after the 'incident'

- if the conflict was unresolved: *there's no hope of agreement, you can't win them all*
- when the conflict was resolved: *I handled that well, that was an improvement.*

Much anger arousal is caused by an individual's poor ability to solve problems. This will be exacerbated at times of high arousal when processing of information is poor. The style of problem-solving thinking shown determines whether the individual perceives a problem as a surmountable task.

2. The arousal component

Once again, self-monitoring of bodily changes, such as increased rate of heart-beat, breathing, sweating and muscle tension, can be helpful not only in raising awareness of the physical effects of anger but also to provide a measure of the extent of arousal against which any change can be measured.

Progressive relaxation techniques (Jacobson 1938) are recommended as the main form of direct arousal reduction. These are introduced early in the course of training so that the individual has the opportunity to learn and practise the relaxation. The intention is that the individual will learn to appreciate the difference between his or her body being tense and being relaxed.

As the skill is developed, the techniques can be applied at times of arousal and also on a regular basis to keep arousal levels generally low. Imagery is used to allow the individual to relax during a well-known provocation. Gradually the individual becomes able to carry out a shortened version of the techniques that he or she can use to complement the less direct methods of reducing arousal, such as self-instruction, cognitive restructuring or modifying the environment.

3. The behavioural component

Training provides an opportunity for individuals to increase their ability to:

(a)   communicate anger in a way that is effective yet not aggressive. This follows the principles of social skills and assertion training (Liberman, DeRisi and Mueser 1989) and includes the verbal and non-verbal components of behaviour.

(b)   use a systematic problem-solving approach when faced with anger arousal: identify the problem objectively, consider possible responses, weigh up the consequences of each alternative and implement the best one, and then evaluate the outcome. This sounds lengthy but, with training and practice, can become a quick process that the individual uses automatically.

All three of the components of skill acquisition are important, but clearly some clients may require a greater emphasis on one aspect of training. For example, some clients do not have the necessary assertion skills and have therefore developed a pattern of aggressive behaviour in order to get their point across. Others may have adequate behavioural skills but are quick to perceive a threat or injustice and react accordingly.

Application training

As the training progresses, the range of situations that the individual finds provoking becomes apparent (through self-monitoring and discussion). This phase of the training uses role-play and homework to allow the individual to practise his or her new coping skills. If the situations are presented in a hierarchical order, i.e. the least provoking leading up to the most provoking, the individual should have the opportunity to cope in increasingly difficult situations. This, in turn, encourages increased confidence, reduces the fear of losing control and consequently improves self-esteem.

Summary of key components

- therapeutic engagement
- client education about anger – functional and dysfunctional
- self-monitoring of anger frequency, intensity and triggers
- provocation hierarchy formed from self-monitoring data, this is used when practising coping skills
- arousal reduction techniques of progressive relaxation, breathing techniques and imagery
- cognitive restructuring by altering attentional focus, modifying appraisals, problem-solving thinking and using self-instruction
- behavioural skill development in communication and assertiveness through role-play
- practising the new skills whilst visualising and role-playing progressively more anger-provoking scenes from the provocation hierachy.

Does the treatment work?

The stress inoculation approach has been found to be effective with a wide range of populations. A review of the literature can be found in Novaco (1994b).

There are, of course, limitations of anger treatments. Some clients are very resistant to change, and those who are seriously disturbed are a particular challenge (Howells 1989). It also has to be acknowledged that some inpatient settings may actually contribute to increased stress and anger levels (Levey and Howells 1991; Black et al. 1997). Environmental changes and education for all members of the treatment team may be required before attempting to implement treatment successfully in such a setting.

ADAPTING THE EXISTING TREATMENT TO SUIT CLIENTS WITH COGNITIVE IMPAIRMENT

Establishing the need

Clearly, when working with those individuals who have cognitive impairment, the above treatment intervention has to be simplified. A number of difficulties are immediately apparent, but others were discovered only as the modified version evolved in practice. These are identified below.

- This group may require preliminary work to cope with the identification, labelling and then articulation of anger. Education on the terms anger and anxiety, and indeed on the normality of emotions in general, will assist the individuals to engage in treatment.
- Extracting the social meaning of a situation by analysing information from other people and the environment (social cognition) is a challenge for this group. Extra training in observation and the importance of non-verbal behaviours will be necessary.
- The cognitive component of the treatment intervention, in particular, is difficult or impossible for some individuals to comprehend. Identifying 'hot cognitions' or potential triggers (and then remembering them) requires both awareness and memory.
- Impaired executive functioning (dysexective syndrome) leading to increased distractability, poor monitoring, attentional and memory defects necessitate a modified style when delivering treatment.

- Acquiring the skills of cognitive reappraisal or alternative interpretation of statements requires a great deal of teaching and, of course, is dependent on well-developed language skills.
- The self-monitoring component can seem an insurmountable hurdle to both the therapist and the individual concerned and consequently is often abandoned.
- The progressive relaxation method used is lengthy and exacting. Individuals may not be able to concentrate for, or attend to, the recommended time of practice (up to an hour) each day.
- In order for the principles of Jacobson to be followed precisely, the user must have sufficient comprehension to follow the specific instructions, and also the powers to discriminate between muscle groups.
- It was found that some individuals disliked the tense and relax procedure. Indeed, some were unable to 'let go' after all the muscle tensing and were more comfortable with a stretching movement such as that described by Mitchell (1977, 1987).
- Some individuals were resistant to participation in any relaxation techniques and refused to associate them with a soaring temper (O'Neill 1997).

Additional influences

So the task was to simplify, yet retain the core components of, the stress inoculation procedure for anger control. This was achieved by looking to the field of learning disability and self-management skill training, as well as applying many practical teaching ideas acquired during clinical practice.

Self-management skill training aims to help the individual to develop his or her internal controls, as does anger management. The core of stress inoculation is self-instruction and this fits comfortably with many of the self-management skills taught to those individuals with learning disabilities. Coping or cue cards – a prompt to take alternative action – are practical ideas from self-management and anxiety management training.

The search for suitable relaxation and arousal reduction techniques was extensive. It included a review of some well-established methods (Mitchell 1977, 1987; Benson 1976, 1985; Payne 1995) but also considered a discrete influence that is a result of personal use of yoga techniques.

A literature search revealed that behavioural relaxation training (BRT) (Schilling and Poppen 1983) has been shown to be effective with those with a mental handicap (Lindsay and Baty 1986a, b; Williams 1990). This method was found to be more easily understood by clients than was abbreviated progressive relaxation training (APR). In BRT the person, who is seated in a comfortable chair rather than lying down, observes and imitates a series of easily demonstrated postures or observable states of relaxation. This procedure acknowledges the reluctance of some individuals to lie down during a group session. It also does not allow the relaxation to be dismissed by the user as a passive activity that has little relevance in those heated moments.

As the relaxation and arousal reduction methods are introduced in the manual, the reader will, therefore, detect influences from many sources. Although methods are suggested, they are by no means prescriptive. Many therapists have a great deal of experience in using relaxation training with their clients and, as such, have determined the methods most suitable.

The evolution of OTSAR

The component of 'On The Spot Arousal Reduction' (see Appendix 1) evolved initially as a way of reducing levels of arousal for clients who were not keen to carry out traditional relaxation. It later proved to meet a need for a practised technique that could be used easily at times of anger arousal.

For some individuals who are resistant to the term relaxation, this form of arousal reduction is a creative way of learning a relaxation response. So OTSAR can be used as an alternative to, or to complement, full relaxation. Luckily the complete title of the technique does not have to be used and the acronym OTSAR revealed itself as a great source of amusement for many clients and fellow occupational therapists or OTs. OTSAR has the potential to be customised and is the result of experience and user feedback.

Summary

This modified version of the stress inoculation procedure for anger control has been used with individuals who have varying degrees of cognitive impairment. Experience has shown that many such individuals are able to recognise increasing levels of anger arousal and can be taught a sequence of events to follow in response to that arousal. Such a sequence would be self-instruction to carry out OTSAR, either to provide a lasting solution, i.e. cooling down and using distraction, or to inhibit the arousal until the individual can seek external help. This process is a 'scaling down' of the cognitive-behavioural model, with the greater emphasis being placed on the behavioural coping skills, whilst still acknowledging the role of the cognitions.

WHICH INDIVIDUALS MIGHT BE SUITABLE FOR ANGER MANAGEMENT?

Initial referral for anger management will invariably come from the treatment team. Before accepting the individual for treatment it is important for the therapist to assess if the referral is appropriate.

Intellectual function

As yet there are no absolute guidelines to cover the level of intellectual function necessary to benefit from the treatment. Previous authors have avoided stating a lower limit, instead looking for evidence of functional ability rather than relying purely on IQ (Black 1990). Black, Cullen and Novaco (1997) assert that people with mild learning disabilities can benefit from cognitive behaviour treatments. This view is backed up by Dagnan and Chadwick (1997), who show that a woman with a full-scale IQ of 65 benefited from cognitive behaviour therapy to treat her depression.

Feindler and Ecton (1986) also state that people with borderline or mild learning disability might benefit from anger control treatment, but consider that the development of the language skills is a far more important factor than IQ.

Memory

Poor memory need not exclude a client from treatment, indeed it is expected that many clients who have cognitive impairment may have some memory problems and strategies to compensate for this will be described in the session plans. However, such a client may be more suited to individual rather than group treatment, to ensure that the pace of delivery can allow for repetition of material.

Language

It appears that without the facility of receptive and expressive language, the individual will not be able to provide themselves with self-guiding statements or self-instruction (Feindler and Ecton 1986). The role of internal speech in developing control of behaviour is described clearly by Goldstein and Keller (1987). They refer to what happens during the course of a child's normal development when, between the ages of 4.5 and 5.5 years, the child's self-verbalisation shifts from overt to covert (internal) speech. Research showing the relationship between impulsivity and poor verbal control of overt behaviour is cited. Hence, self-instruction has been used to train youngsters to provide themselves with internally generated verbal commands.

Williams and Jones (1997) state that the literature provides striking evidence that verbally orientated approaches can help people with learning disabilities, and Black (1990) worked with subjects whose mean mental age was 6 years 5 months when tested by the Peabody Picture Vocabulary Test. So clearly clients with impaired language skills can benefit from the self-instruction component.

Self-instruction strategies have also been used with neurologically impaired adults (O'Callaghan and Couvadelli 1998). However, many clients in this group have multiple cognitive impairments, and language deficits may be compounded by poor memory.

History of behaviour

Information on incidents of aggression and outbursts of anger (obtainable from case notes or incident reports) help to establish what type of aggression the client displays. As stated earlier, it is important to distinguish between angry and instrumental aggression, the latter not being improved by anger management.

Motivation

If a client perceives their anger as a cost, it is likely that they will be at least partly motivated to learn alternative ways of coping. This may be apparent to the treatment team before assessment or it may become clear during the semi-structured interview. If the client shows a glimmer of motivation, further work, such as a cost/benefits exercise and peer group encouragement, may enlighten the client on their choices of response. It also has to be acknowledged that the treatment environment may contribute to a client's motivation to change or not, and this is discussed further in the section 'The treatment setting'.

Ability to self-monitor changes in physiological arousal

Self-monitoring is a necessary part of anger management and leads to written, pictorial or colour-coded records. However, before this recording can take place the client needs to be able to register the change in their levels of arousal. If clients have difficulty with this, a simple biofeedback machine that is worn on a wristband can raise their awareness, as it 'bleeps' each time the arousal increases.

CHECKLIST FOR SUITABILITY

Inclusion

- Any aggression to objects, others or self is fuelled by anger.
- Is distressed by the anger or by the costs of it, such as resulting restrictions, loss of broken belongings, consequences in relationships.
- Shows some motivation to engage in treatment, i.e. wants to 'be in charge' of the anger.
- Often impatient, frustrated and upset by environmental triggers.
- Is consenting to treatment.
- Some degree of literacy is ideal, but not essential.
- May have poor assertion skills.
- May have low self-esteem (see Rosenberg (1965) for measures of self-esteem).

Exclusion

- Shows well-planned, instrumental, rather than angry, aggression.
- Feels his or her anger/aggression pays off and does not want to change.
- Shows active psychosis (such as to interfere with treatment).
- Regular use of drugs/alcohol/solvents.
- Severe memory problems, unable to retain information.
- Language functioning does not permit use of self-instruction.

DURATION OF TREATMENT

Novaco's treatment procedure (updated 1993–4) was originally devised for out-patients and lasted for 12 90-minute sessions. As the procedure has been used with different populations, so the duration of treatment has been adjusted. It is clear that for many clients 12 sessions are not enough. It is also clear that sessions lasting for 90 minutes are too long for many clients. So is it a matter of delivering the original 18 hours of treatment in shorter, perhaps more frequent, bursts? There may be some sense in this, but clearly it is not simply that prescriptive.

For some, 30-minute sessions twice a week will be most suitable. Kellner and Tutin (1995) found that this style of delivery catered for the clients' limited attention span and allowed for frequent repetition and positive reinforcement as skills were acquired. However, if longer sessions can be tolerated they are preferable. There is then adequate time for feedback, and opportunity to cover new material and practise arousal reduction techniques at each session.

A review of the studies published reveals courses of treatment lasting from 8 to 50 sessions (see page 23 for examples). Despite this diversity, the work of Black (1990) and Black and Novaco (1993), as well as personal experience, shows that when working with the cognitively impaired, the speed of delivery has to be adjusted from the original work.

There may be a need to include pre-sessional work that increases the clients' emotional awareness. Some ideas for this are given in page 48. This work primes clients for the main treatment, when they will need to be able to notice, recognise and then self-monitor their anger. An added bonus of this pre-sessional work is that the group members have the opportunity to work together, and hopefully this lays the foundations for self-disclosure, and trust in other members.

Examples of studies, showing the number of treatment sessions:

8–12 sessions Uomoto and Brockway (1992) Two cases of brain-injured patients and their family members

10 sessions Schlichter and Horan (1981) Study with institutionalised juvenile delinquents

12 sessions Wilcox and Dowrick (1992) Study with adolescents; Benson, Rice and Miranti (1986) working with mentally handicapped adults; Lira, Carne and Masri (1983) with a brain-injured man

25 sessions Renwick et al. (1997) Pilot study with forensic hospital patients. Treatment includes a five-session preparatory stage.

28 sessions Black and Novaco (1993) Study of a developmentally handi-capped man

40 sessions Kellner and Tutin (1995) Working with developmentally and emotionally disabled high school students

50 sessions Black (1990) Study with mentally handicapped adults

Further studies are reviewed in Novaco (1994b, 1997)

Hence, it is likely that anger management work may take up to four times longer with those clients who have cognitive impairment. An individual's rate of progress will depend on many participant variables, including:

- intellectual ability
- attention
- memory
- motivation
- difficulties in the processing of information, either the amount or speed. This will affect the speed of delivery, the amount of repetition needed and the necessary environment for delivery (see page 26).

Group sessions present another unpredictable variable, i.e. how well the group gels. If a sound, trusting environment develops, the amount of interaction and support generated within the group will increase. In this case to 'hurry through' the stages of treatment may throw away learning opportunities. This is not to say that the therapist should regard the duration of treatment as open-ended. Regular reviews of progress are essential, but a therapist anxious to keep to a tight timescale risks unnecessary pressure on the members, and is left with the haunting question 'have the clients absorbed the session material?'

REMEMBER, SLOW BUT SURE!

Other skill-building sessions may complement the work done in anger management. These are: relaxation, problem-solving, social skills and assertion training (see Figure opposite). Often clients are also involved in some of these anyway, but if not, a course of sessions could be offered as a change, or indeed respite, from a long course of anger management!

Follow-up

Experience has shown that regular follow-up sessions (say monthly) help to reinforce the knowledge and the newly acquired skills. Some individuals seem to need a regular 'top-up' as a maintenance dose of treatment. There is further information on 'bringing the techniques out of the treatment room' and maintaining skills after the course of treatment on page 125.

Components of anger management

PROBLEM
SOLVING

ASSERTION
TRAINING

STRESS INOCULATION
TRAINING

SOCIAL SKILLS
TRAINING

S I T

R
E
L
A
X
A
T
I
O
N

L
E
I
S
U
R
E

GROUP OR INDIVIDUAL TREATMENT?

The cognitive-behavioural techniques of anger management are now used with an increasing range of clients. There are reports of the treatment being delivered both in groups and on an individual basis (reviewed in Novaco 1994b). Yet how does the therapist decide which is the most suitable for the client?

The treatment is most commonly carried out in group settings of between three and eight members. The advantages are as follows:

- It is a cost-effective method of delivery.
- It is ideal for some of the techniques, such as role-play and assertion training. The group also helps members appreciate the normality of anger as they listen to the perspective of others. Members may find it reassuring to hear that others also experience problematic anger, and that they too are struggling to manage it in an effective way.
- Peers are able to give realistic feedback and reinforcement (this is particularly so if the therapist is working with clients of a different age group or culture from her own).
- Given time, group support can develop and, if it does, this can also be powerful even outside the group.

However, there are some potential disadvantages:

- Clients may not disclose details of their own anger patterns as readily in a group. Many clients can be mistrustful both of other clients and of staff members in the group, particularly if the treatment setting is a secure environment. Possible distrust must be taken into account when asking clients to disclose details of their own anger, which for many people leads to a feeling of betrayal and vulnerability when defences are down. If there is an audience at the time of the disclosure, the person may perceive threat or deny the existence of feelings.

- A trusting therapeutic relationship is the key to clients engaging in treatment, so it is important to set a gentle, non-threatening treatment environment. In some cases this may be achieved only on an individual basis, either initially, or for the course of treatment.

- When anger management is carried out on an individual basis, if possible complement the work by offering skill-building groups, such as social skills, assertion training or problem-solving. These groups will provide an opportunity to develop the interpersonal skills needed to express anger effectively.

- The cognitive aspects of anger are very personal and clients may feel that they are not suitable to be unearthed in a group. When clients are living together in the same hospital or community setting, the focus of their anger may be another client in the group. If they report this anger in the group they may fear retaliation outside the session. Conversely, some clients could attempt to use the group as a public reporting place where they can shame or antagonise other members.

- If more in-depth cognitive restructuring work is necessary, the therapist may choose to do this on an individual basis, but in addition to the group sessions.

- Some clients have difficulty processing more than one stimulus at any one time and therefore cannot focus their attention if they are in a noisy or busy group setting. Experience has shown that if this is the case the environmental setting for the delivery of treatment is of paramount importance, and therefore it may be more productive to work individually. (Good work has been wasted because it was delivered in a distracting setting and consequently not attended to; the client having no recollection of it later on.)

So for some, a group may not be appropriate or even available. If this is the case, the principles can be followed on an individual basis, although the behavioural skill-building component may have to be adapted within the session and practised, *in vivo*, outside the treatment room.

THERAPISTS

Experience

If treatment is to be delivered in groups, it is necessary to have a regular therapist and co-therapist. It is expected that the therapist, at least, will have developed a knowledge of cognitive-behavioural techniques such as anxiety management, and will have undertaken wider reading on the subject of anger and its management. Ideally the therapist should have undertaken additional training on anger management. However, if this has not been possible, any experience gained in running skill-building groups, such as social skills training, assertion or problem-solving is relevant because these are all components of anger management (see Figure 1 on page 25). These ideals naturally also apply to the therapist who is working on an individual basis.

Whether group or individual treatment is delivered, therapists will need to learn the specific cognitive-behavioural techniques of stress inoculation. They will also need to have a regular supervision time in which to discuss cases, the therapeutic relationship, and receive objective input on any problematic situations.

Self-awareness

It is advisable for the therapist to spend time considering his or her understanding of anger both in themselves and others. Any therapist delivering anger management treatment will be exposed to a great deal of anger expressed both orally and in written form in diaries. Anger arousal can be infectious, therefore, when working in close proximity to clients who are communicating their levels of anger; it is wise to remember that this process can evoke strong feelings within those who are listening. The therapist is no exception to this and will, like everyone else, have his or her own anger triggers. If the therapist either identifies with, or is too distressed by, the anger reported by others, his or her own personal feelings could potentially affect the delivery of treatment and the therapeutic relationship.

The therapist should ask himself or herself the following questions:

- What do I mean by anger? Consider semantics and labelling.
- Am I clear about the difference between anger and aggression?
- Have I thought about my own views on anger and its expression? These will depend on experience, upbringing, culture and religion.
- Is anger ever justified?
- Is anger always wrong or is it useful?
- Am I aware of my own anger triggers?
- What is my attitude towards a client who has shown a lot of anger and/or aggression towards others?
- Am I judgemental or do I have an understanding (though not necessarily approval) of others' anger?
- Will any disgust of a client's previous behaviour affect the therapeutic relationship?
- Am I prepared to listen to reports of anger – some will be about other staff members – and can I remain impartial?

CHECKLIST FOR SUITABILITY

Before setting up an anger management group it is necessary to have identified a regular therapist and co-therapist. Both will need skill to:

- maintain the focus of the group
- be flexible during sessions to ensure a balance between covering planned session material and capitalising on useful learning situations that arise during the feedback
- develop a knack of eliciting the key points in feedback
- interpret the comments of the group members without altering their meaning
- observe group dynamics and reactions as anger-evoking situations are discussed or re-enacted
- organise role-play, using video equipment if it is available
- be a facilitator and a teacher, using active listening skills
- be mindful of the importance of the therapeutic relationship, particularly if working on an individual basis
- be resourceful and unshockable!

LISTENING TO A PERSON REPORTING THEIR ANGER

Remember that any 'hot cognitions' reported in a session were, at the time of anger arousal, real to the person concerned. Many of these cognitions may be distorted, hence the person's need for anger management training. A therapist must not adopt a defensive response when listening, as this will inhibit the client's reporting and recording.

Hints:
*   Listen to the person's point of view and try to put yourself in their place.
*   Do not become immediately defensive (from then on you won't hear properly).
*   However illogical it may sound, this is what the person was thinking at the time.
*   When in an angry **STATE** the person really believes that they are in the right; that is therefore not the best time to challenge.
*   Encourage reporting of facts rather than venting of anger.
*   Encourage the person to reduce their level of arousal before confronting any problems.
*   Acknowledge that you can accept that that is what they felt (it doesn't mean you have to agree with it!).

Don't say:
*   *I know how you feel!*
*   *Now calm down!*
*   *Take a deep breath.*
*   *You are not the only person to have problems.*
*   *Don't be silly!*

Instead, try statements such as:

- *You have had a bad time and now this seems to be the last straw for you.*
- *I can see that you are upset/angry (use their word).*
- *It's not really me you are angry with, is it?*
- *Take your time and tell me what happened.*
- *So it all started when...*
- *Well, it does sound as if you could have a point there.*
- *Let me help you to get over this intense feeling and then we can think it through (turning the energy towards solving the problem).*
- *Take one step at a time.*

If possible, encourage the person to:

- Sit down. However, they may not want to sit down, they may see it as 'backing down' or 'giving in', or they may be too aroused to settle.
- Use any breathing techniques that you know they have learned previously, e.g. diaphragmatic breathing.
- Breathe out or sigh, then take two deep breaths – *breathe away the anger.*

At the end of the communication stand up slowly and do not make any hasty movements for they could be perceived as threatening.

DE-ESCALATION TECHNIQUES

When faced with an angry person and if you can sense the warning signs:

- Look for an exit (discreetly).
- Stay out of the person's space.
- Do not make sudden moves. It can appear threatening and remember, they may be frightened too.
- If you want to move don't just step back, instead make a side turn.
- Keep an open posture.
- Breathe slowly – be aware of your own level physiological arousal.
- Think calmly.
- Encourage the person to distance themselves from the provoking cues.
- Stay calm – don't argue back.
- Keep an even tone of voice.
- Set limits, e.g. *Let's take a few minutes to cool down, and then we will try to solve it.*
- 'When the anger is up, the judgement is down', so this is not the best time for reasoning.
- Even an apology can be misinterpreted at this state of arousal; in fact an urgent repeated apology can seem like a provocation!

Remember:

- An angry person is quick to perceive threat, harm or injustice.
- Their attentional focus is primed to look for it!
- Cognitive processing is at its worst at times of arousal.

THE THERAPEUTIC RELATIONSHIP

Establishing a common goal

If the treatment is to be effective, there is a need for both the therapist and the client to have a common goal of treatment. This may be quickly established if anger is a problem to the client because it causes them distress or if the perceived or actual costs of the anger weigh heavily.

Yet even if a client accepts that anger is a problem to them, their initial plan may not be to change their own anger, but instead to try to change those people with whom they are angry, i.e. the others! A common expression is: *Yes I do get angry and it's a problem, but they cause it so they must change, not me!*

Whilst we have to acknowledge that anger can be a natural warning sign that something is unfair or a violation, it can also be a sign that a person's appraisal of a situation is biased or irrational. To then place the blame on others is a common external attribution. This might be comfortable to live with but it does not encourage the client to take any responsibility for their emotion and behaviour. Such an attribution may be voiced frequently in the early stages of treatment and it highlights both the client's fear of change and their lack of understanding about the management of problematic anger. They may assume that they will be expected never to feel angry and to extinguish all expression of anger, thus leaving them to be seen as a 'pushover', rather than learning to evaluate the anger more carefully and, if it is justified, to assert their views. Hence there needs to be a collaborative process of discovery which contributes to forming the therapeutic alliance.

It is worth noting that clients who have a poor memory may be inclined to feel angry either with themselves or with others whom they believe have taken advantage of them. This can hinder the setting of a common goal until the deficit is acknowledged and the necessary memory strategies are adopted.

The therapeutic alliance

One of the assumptions associated with cognitive behaviour therapy is that clients can engage in a collaborative relationship within the first few sessions. When working with an angry client this is not easily fulfilled. It may take much longer than it would with a client being treated for other emotional problems, and happen only after considerable effort on behalf of the therapist. Yet it is necessary to achieve this if any thorough work is to be done.

DiGiuseppe, Tarfrate and Eckhardt (1994) talk about the necessity of establishing a therapeutic alliance between client and therapist. This alliance is more than the therapeutic relationship that is referred to in psychotherapy, and includes an agreement between therapist and client on the goals and tasks of therapy. DiGiuseppe (1995) states that this agreement can sometimes be difficult to reach with an angry client who may hold certain beliefs, about himself or others, that make a need to change seem unnecessary. For example:

- *I must express my anger in order to get rid of it.* This belief that cathartic release is effective as a way of reducing arousal is not supported by research (Tavris 1989). In fact 'talking it out' or directing it at something or somebody, often prolongs or increases the arousal unless followed by some reappraisal of the cause of the anger.
- *People should never be late!* Such 'should, ought and must' statements are often seen as rules for life, but if followed to the extreme can be unforgiving, unrealistic and lead to anger.
- *If you don't show your anger you're weak and a pushover!* This belief is commonly held if the client was raised in an environment where adults showed anger in order to discipline, so no shouting meant no power.

Such beliefs may hinder a client's motivation to change and the forming of a therapeutic alliance. These beliefs will have to be discovered and then gently challenged in a way that will not cause the client threat or alienation. The therapist will need to decide if this is in a group setting or, more likely, individually. The former can give group support whilst what are often commonly held beliefs about anger are dispelled; the latter offers an opportunity for in-depth understanding at a pace ideal for the client. At all times, the therapist has to show empathy with the client, hence allowing for disclosure without judgement.

THE TREATMENT SETTING

Anger must be viewed contextually (Novaco 1993), therefore the effect of the environment in which the client lives must never be underestimated. It will provide its own set of dynamics that may, in turn, be evident within the treatment setting. The therapist needs to remember the implications of this when treating clients who are living: (a) in an institution, perhaps detained under a section of the Mental Health Act 1983, or (b) in the community.

Each of these settings will have its own set of social rules and values, expectations and perhaps even prejudices. It is therefore worth acknowledging that there will be both costs and benefits of treating clients in either setting. The costs, or potential problems, are outlined below. The benefits are the opposite of the costs and are therefore not listed.

Potential problems of working within an institution

- During initial assessment, clients may not disclose the full extent of their anger and aggression in case it results in increased staff observation or restrictions.
- Clients may have a deep sense of mistrust of members of staff because they will be seen as part of a powerful system. Davis and Boster (1992) point out that the client has to learn to trust and not fear the clinician, but in a secure residential setting clinicians do not fully trust clients and clients do not fully trust clinicians. Consequently it may take longer to establish therapeutic alliance (see page 35).
- Clients detained under a section of the Mental Health Act will feel disempowered and naturally this will affect the balance in the collaborative relationship.
- The delicate balance between the needs of the clients, therapeutic requirements and security needs (Renwick et al. 1997) can mean that

the therapist may feel that he or she cannot please both the client and the institutional staff.

- It can be difficult for clients to attempt to practise new skills in an environment that is rife with undue provocations. The interactions between clients can be unpredictable, to say the least, and may not reinforce the practice of a new skill. If a client discovers that others do not respond to an assertive request, he or she may resort to his or her previous pattern of aggression.

- Provocative interactions need not be confined to clients. Levey and Howells (1991), who argue that much of the aggression that occurs in inpatient settings (both forensic and psychiatric) is anger-mediated, state that interactions between staff and clients can also be provocative. Although some of this could be intentional, we have to assume that much is caused by entrenched ill-informed attitudes and behaviours. An early study by Schlichter and Horan (1981) refers to staff undermining the efficacy of the stress inoculation treatment. However, Levey and Howells (1991) assert that some of these problems can be avoided by staff training.

- The physical environment of a locked ward (i.e. lack of privacy and peace) may not be conducive to practising arousal reduction techniques.

- It can be difficult to carry out stage 3 of the treatment when clients are detained and therefore do not have access to the provocations that were high on their original hierarchical list.

- It is very important how the sessions are regarded, both by those who attend and also by fellow clients, members of the treatment team, family, carers or any other people who are influential on the client. As Feindler (1991) states, 'it is important to continue to ensure that it is *not* perceived as a punitive group for trouble makers'.

Potential problems of working in a community setting

- It can be difficult to make direct observational records to back up any self-report data.

- The therapist or team may find it difficult to give support between sessions.

- It can be difficult to reinforce new learning and use of techniques.

- How can one give a prompt to do homework?

- Attendance at centres where the treatment is delivered can be erratic (dependent on transport, etc.), i.e. the audience is not captive.

FACILITIES

- A suitable group room with comfortable chairs.
- Whiteboard and pens.
- Supply of writing materials/clipboards.
- Visual aids as mentioned in the manual.
- Video equipment – VCR and camcorder.

Key point

For anger management to be successful, it is important that individuals engage fully in treatment. This can present a conflict if the treatment has been prescribed for the person by the team and yet the person still regards his or her anger as a benefit rather than a cost to himself or herself. Cultivate an atmosphere that is relaxing and friendly. It is not easy for many people to focus on their anger and resulting behaviours, which may lead to loss of control, fear or guilt. Therefore, the more conducive the setting is to participation, the better. Promote a sense of privilege about being in the group, it is not suitable for everyone, but only those who are willing to work hard at learning to 'be boss of' their anger.

Safety precautions

Not suprisingly, clients who attend anger management sessions have a propensity to become angry, and therapists may feel that they are an unpredictable group to work with. This could potentially cause the therapist alarm, and inhibit the treatment process. Therefore, it is both advisable and reassuring to have in place a number of strategies to provide security to both the therapist and the clients. Discuss these as part of the introduction session.

- Agree, with clients, a plan of action that can be used if they become agitated, i.e. if clients become aware of their own increasing levels of arousal they may leave the session and 'take 5' before returning to continue. As already stated, it is likely that as high levels of arousal are recounted, clients may become agitated. During the early part of the treatment the 'take 5' routine may be the only coping strategy the clients have.
- Let it be known what response will be made if the worst scenario (aggression) is shown. Depending on the treatment setting there may be an existing procedure that could be used if a client, or clients, become disturbed.

It is wise for the therapist to be aware of de-escalation techniques described on page 33.

ASSESSMENT AND EVALUATION

Effective assessment and evaluation of treatment can be carried out only if adequate information is collected. It is ideal if the therapist can design and set up a system for collecting data from a variety of sources. If this system is established before treatment begins, there will then be a framework in place for collecting baseline data and measuring any future change. Four methods of data collection are described below. This is followed by some suggestions for the methods that can be used for pre-treatment (baseline data) collection, the ongoing collection and post-treatment data collection.

Methods of data collection

1. Archival records

This is information on incidents of aggression and outbursts of anger; it can be obtained from case notes or incident reports.

2. Self-report measures

Self-report measures, such as: the State-Trait Anger Expression Inventory (Spielberger 1988); the Buss–Perry Aggression Questionnaire (Buss and Perry 1992); or the Children's Anger Response Checklist CARC (Feindler et al. 1993, cited in Feindler 1995), are traditionally used before commencing anger management treatment. Self-report is used because anger is a subjective emotion and therefore cannot accurately be reported on by anyone other than the person experiencing it.

However, reference must be made to the vulnerabilities of self-report measures, not least with a subject who has cognitive impairment. First, the existing measures are not validated with this population and, second, the subject's language and literacy skills may pose problems. So whereas the Novaco Anger Scale (NAS) was previously recommended (O'Neill 1995) as a pre-treatment measure, it will be too complex for many of those with cognitive impairment, and if it is used, it must be thought of as a helpful addition to a semi-structured interview, rather than a reliable tool for research. There are, nevertheless, benefits in using a self-report measure, Benson et al. (1986) used a modified version of the Finch children's inventory of anger. During the process of using such a measure the therapist is able to appreciate more fully the client's awareness of emotions, insight and likelihood of engagement. This is the essential first step of the collaborative process.

Diaries provide a valuable source of data. This is, of course, dependent on the client's literacy skills and motivation, but pictorial diaries and an incentive scheme to record can overcome this hurdle.

3. Direct observational recording

This is the most objective and comprehensive assessment strategy. It is completed by those having most contact with the client and can be used successfully to record overt behaviours such as any aggression. It cannot, however, be used with success to record the subjective emotional state of anger itself.

Because many clients referred for anger management have problems with aggression, direct observational recording is relevant and is an invaluable and reliable source of behavioural data. Suitable methods of recording are: straightforward ABC, Antecedent, Behaviour, Consequence, charts (described very clearly by Murphy and Clare 1991); an 'in-house' behavioural recording sheet; or a behavioural inventory, such as the MOAS, Modified Overt Aggression Scale (Alderman, Knight and Morgan 1997). MOAS classifies behaviours by type and severity, and will therefore show any change in the pattern of aggression, for example hitting the wall instead of other people. Results provide a weighted severity and frequency of aggression.

To ensure reliability of such recording it is necessary for observers to have adequate training both on the rationale of the recording and the technique itself (Feindler and Ecton 1986).

4. Semi-structured interview

See page 45.

Pre-treatment gathering of information

If it is decided that the individual is suitable for treatment, you should collect baseline data. This will allow the measurement of change by:

- archival records
- self-report measures
- diaries. Howells (1989) suggests asking clients, and a significant other, to collect data for two weeks before treatment commences
- direct observational recording, e.g. ABC charts or MOAS
- semi-structured interview (see page 45)
- biofeedback to monitor levels of physiological arousal.

Gathering this will contribute to the therapist's understanding of the client and assist treatment planning to include individual needs.

Ongoing collection of data

Feindler and Ecton (1986) describe clearly the need for this. Specific target behaviours can be clearly defined and data collected on incidents of aggression or angry outbursts from:

- the client's case notes
- oral self-report or diaries; the style of diary may change as treatment progresses
- direct observational recording (DOR) using an 'in-house' recording sheet, ABC charts or MOAS
- physiological measures, e.g. pulse rate or blood pressure before and after relaxation, or biofeedback to assist self-monitoring of arousal levels.

These data are relatively easy to collect in an institutional setting where staff are primed to observe and record. In other settings, family members or carers may be willing to use simple recording methods to back up self-report data.

Evaluation of treatment

At the end of treatment, data comparable to that collected pre-treatment should be collected. Comparison of the data will provide simple quantitative statistics. Bellack and Hersen (1984) offer information on single case study designs and on group evaluations.

SEMI-STRUCTURED INTERVIEW

The purpose of the semi-structured interview is to:

- contribute to discovering the individual's pattern of anger

- assess the person's degree of self-awareness, acceptance and general attitude towards his or her anger

- highlight an individual's desire or reluctance to manage his or her anger

- establish the first step of collaborative work.

The interview

- Explain the role of therapist.
- Explain that anger is a perfectly normal emotion but that we often do not understand it properly. Different people will get angry over different things; it is not the same for everyone. Sometimes getting angry can cause problems for us or others. Ask, 'would you agree with that?'
- Sometimes people need some helpful tips on managing their anger. Refer to anger management sessions (the client may know that others attend).
- Ask if you can try to see what it is like for the client.

Establish awareness and pattern of anger

The following questions are suggested; they are not prescriptive.

- What are some of the things that make you angry?

- What might make you very angry? And just a little bit angry? (Can client grade degree of anger?)

- Can you tell me what it's like for you when you get angry?
- Have you felt angry recently?
- When was that? Can you tell me about that?
- Does it happen often? (establish frequency).
- Do you get any warning signs? So what might happen?
- Would other people know that you were getting angry? How might they tell?

Body

- When you are angry does your body get tense or unsettled? Where in particular?
- Is your sleep affected?

Thoughts

- Does getting angry change the way you think? (can't concentrate, think hateful thoughts, set expectations of others/self?).
- Do you think a lot about what made you angry? (rumination).
- Does that go on for a long time? (duration).

Behaviour

- What might you do when you are angry? (shout, slam, smash things, sulk, self-harm?).

Influences

- Are there some places where you are more likely to get angry?
- Are there some places where you are less likely to get angry?
- Does it make any difference who is there?
- What might make it worse? (conditions – heat, noise, hunger).
- What can you do to calm yourself down? Does it help?
- Do you know of anything else that might help?

Costs/benefits

- So how do you view/regard your anger? (distress; fear; great, no problem!).

- Does it get you what you want?

- Does it get you into trouble?

- After you have been angry do you ever wish you had reacted differently? – any regrets?

- What do your friends and family think of it?

- What do they say when you get angry?

- Would it be worth trying to learn more skills so that you can be in charge of your anger?

- Would you have any concerns about changing your ways?

If yes, ask the last question:

- Why, what might happen? Can you think of ways that you could lose out?

Plan for future treatment

As a result of the pre-treatment gathering of information and the semi-structured interview, the therapist has to decide if the client is ready to commence treatment immediately. It may be decided that the individual would benefit from some pre-sessional work aimed at increasing emotional awareness and self-awareness (see page 48). If the client appears reluctant to see the reason for the treatment, the use of motivational interviewing methods (Miller and Rollnick 1991) may be helpful.

If the client does seem ready for anger management, which format would be most suitable for their needs:

- group sessions?

- individual sessions?

- group plus some individual to 'top up' the cognitive work?

- how many? Agree initial number and review later.

Always involve the client in the negotiation so as to work collaboratively.

PRE-SESSIONAL WORK TO INCREASE EMOTIONAL AWARENESS

It very common for clients to have difficulty in recognising and encoding emotions. Most of us are able to identify a range of emotions well before school age. However, learning disability, acquired brain injury, or very disturbed early years may lead to a deficit in emotional awareness. When a client experiences an intense feeling of emotion yet cannot understand it's meaning, or how to label it, it is no wonder that they are not able to regulate the emotion or express it effectively and with dignity.

Yet in order to appreciate the work in anger management it is necessary to be able to recognise and label emotions, particularly anger. So for those who need extra time to develop emotional awareness, the following ideas may be useful:

- Look at photographs of famous people depicting various emotions.
- Take photographs of the clients showing various emotions.
- Watch videos of television soaps – these usually contain a great deal of emotion!
- For those who find drawing an easier way to express themselves try books such as Draw on your Emotions (Sunderland and Engleheart 1994).

Discuss the different words that people use to describe emotions. There may be variations in language depending upon age, and cultural background. Session 1 includes the semantics of anger, and how it differs from aggression, but preparatory work may be needed to clarify the meaning of 'angry type words' versus other emotional words. People may have very different views of the value or need for the varying emotions. For example, anger may be viewed negatively, whereas anxiety, on the other hand, may command tolerance and sympathy. Encourage clients to analyse what they saw by asking questions such as:

- Who was angry/sad/happy?
- Why do you think he/she is angry/sad/happy?
- How angry/sad/happy do you think they are? Start to introduce the concept of measuring emotions. Keep it simple at this stage, e.g. a lot or a little.
- What do you think he/she is feeling in his/her body?
- I wonder what he/she might be thinking?
- What might happen to him/her as a result of getting angry/sad/happy?

Discuss the topic and gradually raise the awareness of emotions in general. An emotional-awareness assessment measure was developed by Reed and Clements (1989) for use with adolescents and young adults with learning disability.

THE WAY THE MANUAL WORKS

The manual has been designed as a working document for use by fellow therapists and health professionals. The material is copyright, but permission is granted for the user to photocopy the pages indicated for use with clients only. No other parts of this document may be reproduced without the written consent of the author. If information is referred to for any purpose other than treatment sessions, the author requests that reference be given to the document.

Although some background information has been given at the beginning of the manual, further reading is suggested. References for the text and those of additional interest are contained at the end of the manual.

The natural sequence of the three-stage stress inoculation anger control treatment will be followed in the manual. However, the rate of progress originally suggested has been amended to suit the needs of those clients with limited cognitive ability. As explained earlier, the three stages – cognitive preparation, skill acquisition phase and application training – are, in practice, interrelated within the treatment sessions. The first part of training actually starts with assessment and the semi-structured interview. It also includes any pre-sessional work to increase emotional awareness, should this be necessary before establishing, and learning about, the individual's pattern of anger. Therefore, the background information about anger has to be passed on to the client *before* the skill training begins. With this group of individuals the trick is to impart that information whilst being mindful that 'chalk and board' techniques may not be effective.

Hence the standard delivery has been adapted. Rather than three distinct phases, the first seven session plans concentrate on the cognitive prepar-ation, and the rest on skill acquisition and application training. It is important to remember that although session plans are numbered, there may be considerable variation in the rate of progress when working through the course.

It could be necessary to take more than one session to cover a plan. For this reason, it may be helpful to view each plan as a block rather than as an individual session.

The frequency of sessions is not prescribed but, in practice, one per week is commonplace, although for some clients more frequent sessions may be appropriate. For the purpose of this manual, sessions will be referred to as occurring weekly.

Each session plan/outline is presented in a consistent format:

- feedback
- practical work
- relaxation
- homework.

Additional theoretical knowledge on the topic is provided in 'Therapist's Notes'.

Speech is denoted by the use of italics. Examples would be statements or questions used by the therapist, or self-instructional speech used as a result of anger arousal.

For the benefit of the therapist, the first few session plans include a good deal of explanation; as a consequence, the early plans are considerably longer than later ones.

Also included in the manual are:

- plans of additional sessions if extra learning/practice is required
- additional information on arousal reduction methods
- resources for use in sessions – hand-outs
- diaries
- worksheets – there are two versions of each, a blank to be used by the client and a completed worksheet to be used as a teaching aid or prompt by the therapist
- feedback sheets.

SESSIONS

SESSION 1

Welcome

Introduce the therapists and members of the group to each other. A cup of tea or coffee can be an inviting extra incentive to attend.

Introduction

To introduce the idea of anger management the therapist may ask the following question:

Do we all get angry? Maybe we call it something else.

- Allow the group to suggest other words for anger: rage, mad, pissed off, furious, wound-up, 'on your toes', etc.

- Compare the likelihood of getting angry with that of getting anxious, afraid or other normal emotions.

Practical

Let's find out what makes us angry.

Divide into two groups and work with a large sheet of paper to brainstorm – *what makes us angry?* Examples are given in the box below.

WHAT MAKES US ANGRY?

Not being able to do what you want
People taking the mickey
Being hurt
People not understanding what you're trying to say
Being accused of something
People staring at you
Memories
Queuing
People referring to your bad past

(Keep the sheet of paper to refer to later)

At this stage there may be a great deal of confusion between anger and aggression. Explain the difference briefly if necessary, but this will be clarified later. Do not issue too much theory in any one session, particularly the first.

Feedback

Draw out that perhaps we do all get angry and that it is quite normal to get angry sometimes.

> This is necessary because many people feel it is wrong to get angry, they may have been scolded for it as a child, and consequently have learned to relabel or deny the feeling until the anger arousal is out of control.

But anger can have a **bad** side if, as a result of it, we:

- do or say things we regret
- hurt others or ourselves
- get into trouble
- lose out on privileges/opportunities
- lose friends
- feel bad about ourselves.

Explain

1.   These sessions will help to teach us what to do when we feel angry so that we can remain in charge of the anger, rather than allowing the anger to take us over.

2.   The sessions are **NOT** about taking the anger away, we all need it sometimes to tell us that things are not right; give examples, such as someone going into your room to steal something, being threatened or hurt. Refer to some other justifiable causes of anger that were given in the brainstorming exercise and use them as examples.

3.   The sessions are about learning to see anger as a 'warning sign' on which to take a different action. Introduce the 'take 5' routine (see page 41) to use as a response to arrest increasing arousal levels. In the early stages of treatment this may be the only strategy the clients have to use.

Note: These points may need to be reiterated regularly in sessions.

Stress the one important rule in the group:

NO VIOLENCE

Therapists should decide on a strategy that will be followed if there is any physical aggression shown. The priority is to maintain a safe environment. It may be necessary to stop proceedings and request that the individuals involved leave the group; or, separate the antagonists, distract the group from the disruption, and continue with the session. Do not discuss the incident until the person has had a cooling down period, then, if he or she is willing, try to establish the reason for the upset and consider if there were alternative ways of reacting.

Expectations

Finish by explaining the expectations of the group, that each week:

- we shall all attend sessions, and specify the time, say 40 minutes or one hour long
- we shall do practical work in small groups
- we shall use video. Ask if members have used it before (make it sound fun)
- members will practise what they have learned in a session – use the word 'homework' if that seems appropriate
- there will be contact with the individual's key worker if applicable
- we shall finish with a 'winding down', relaxing time.

By the end of this session it is hoped that the group will:

- have enjoyed the session!
- intend to come next week (commitment)
- have some understanding of what will be expected of them
- have heard of the normality of anger as well as the problems associated with it.

Therapist's notes

Anger is very personal, and different for each of us; it depends on an individual's standards, attitudes and beliefs (see Novaco model cited in O'Neill 1995). Often the current event that triggers the anger response is linked to our past memories (old tapes), as well as our beliefs and expectations about what 'should' and 'ought' to happen.

The exercise in this session helps both the individual concerned and the therapist learn about the individual's patterns of anger, in readiness to spot potential triggers in future.

SESSION 2

Welcome

Recap

In last week's session we agreed:

- that we all get angry sometimes
- that some of us call it something else
- that different things make us angry (it may be useful to produce the brainstorming list from last week's session as a reminder)
- anger is a normal emotion, but it can have a bad side
- how the sessions will help us
- expectations of the group.

Practical

Now work towards learning what people **DO** when they are angry. Brainstorm ideas – examples may be, shout, throw things, clench fists, hit people or the wall, make rude signs, swear, sulk, run away, self-harm, pace around. Hopefully there will be some adaptive behaviours suggested as well. Highlight the differences between the two types of behaviour.

- Some of these will no doubt be aggressive, so now clarify the difference between anger and aggression (see below).
- Refer to the brainstorming ideas, and pull out a few examples of anger and aggression to illustrate the point.

ANGER	is an emotion we 'feel', it's personal and can't really be seen by others.
AGGRESSION	on the other hand, is different. It is the 'doing part' that others can see, hear, feel or report on. It is not acceptable and can lead to trouble and/or pain to others or ourselves.

Now the therapist may ask:

- *do they always go together?*
- *does anger always lead to aggression?*
- *do we have to be angry to be aggressive?*

Give examples of occasions where aggression is not necessarily caused by anger; for example, football hooligans who throw and smash things along with the crowd, or indeed how any of us could show instrumental aggression without being angry. The therapist may wish to give an example of this by dashing into the room, banging the furniture about and throwing things. He or she could then explain that he or she was not angry but wanting a response! This is also good as an icebreaker!

- *So you don't have to be angry to be aggressive.*
- *Some people have just learned that aggression pays off!*
- *It gets them what they want – or does it?*

Discuss

NOT ALL AGGRESSION IS CAUSED BY ANGER

AND ANGER NEED NOT LEAD TO AGGRESSION

There is a choice, and these sessions will teach us skills so that we have a choice of ways to behave when angry.

Relaxation/arousal reduction

So today we have shown how being ANGRY, FIZZING, BOILING 'winds us up' and so we must learn how to wind down!

- Introduce the habit of finishing the session by using simple relaxation techniques, start with calming breaths (see Appendix 1).

We are often told to keep calm, but how do we do that?

A good way is to take control of our breathing. This will help us to:

- reduce any body tension
- concentrate on something apart from what is making us angry
- give us time to think before we speak or shout!

Homework

Introduce the idea of self-monitoring. It may take a while to establish the practice but encourage members to:

- record how many times they got angry in a day/week
- record the intensity on a scale of 0–10

Further, you may

- use the word 'homework' if appropriate
- grade your expectations according to the members' ability
- issue simple, pictorial if necessary, diaries (see Appendix 4).

Practise how to do the homework. Inform and involve relevant staff so as to gain their support and practical help. Provide each client with a folder so that they can keep their personal data (diaries, hand-outs, coping strategies, etc.) and feel a sense of ownership in the treatment.

Therapist's notes on self-monitoring

In general, people are not in the habit of monitoring their behaviour or feelings, and therefore self-monitoring is a task that is foreign to most. It is a complex pattern of behaviour and involves recognition and awareness of the behaviour or emotion to be monitored, as well as the recording process itself. Both of these aspects may lead to problems, and individuals may need to be trained both to discriminate and record incidents of anger arousal.

Yet self-recording is a useful monitoring device for recording incidents of anger, which is a subjective emotion, and can be accurately reported on only by the individual concerned. The act of self-recording can be an intervention in its own right (Pope and Jones 1996). For if it raises awareness of the anger, so that recordings can be made; this can, in turn, influence the sequence of events. So if possible try to encourage at least some degree of self-monitoring, which should develop increased self-awareness. There is great scope for creativity and ingenuity when devising a recording system for patients with poor literacy skills, e.g. wrist counters, 'making a mark' on a picture of an angry person, putting a symbol on a chart, moving a button or a counter from one pocket to another each time there is an incident of anger arousal and then counting up at the end of a given period (staff assistance may be needed).

Diaries help to build up a picture of anger patterns, which allows both the therapist and the individual to learn the potential triggers. They also provide 'real' situations to role-play.

Individuals will need encouragement and help while the habit of self-monitoring develops. Discuss with the participants when and how they will self-monitor and practise the behaviour using role-play. Remember, failure to complete self-monitoring and diaries is often not due to lack of motivation or poor compliance, rather it is expecting a specific skill that has to be learned. Therefore, be encouraging about any recording in order to shape the behaviour.

Note: many points will need repeated explanation, particularly whilst learning about the individuals' patterns of anger.

SESSION

3

Welcome

Check homework

- Ask if anyone kept a record of the frequency and/or the intensity of their anger incidents.
- Praise **ANY** recording, be encouraging! (keep records).

There are obvious weaknesses in self-reporting, whether written or oral, but it is an important part of the training and self-monitoring.

It is helpful to try to cultivate a setting in which individuals feel they can report back honestly without judgement being passed or fear of any consequences. It is wise also to get feedback of behaviours from keyworkers if possible. Decide with them how this will be possible. It is likely that you may have to design a quick and easy-to-use recording system that will be both practical and accurate for staff to use.

Feedback

- Start to develop the habit of each person reporting on incidents of anger. Refer to any self-monitoring, if it is available, or rely on oral feedback if not. In this case you may like to fill in the diary during this session.
- Encourage reports from each person on incidents that:

  - they handled well, i.e. started to feel arousal but managed to keep control
  - became aroused, angry and/or aggressive, and lost control.

- Offer praise for the former and support/reassurance/optimism for the latter!
- Try to be encouraging and positive. Remember, anger is often associated with poor self-esteem. Anger may be accompanied by feelings of punishment and guilt; it is important that a firm yet optimistic attitude is fostered to encourage honesty and co-operation.

Recap

Recap on the main points of last week's session:

- that people may **DO** different things when they are angry
- the difference between anger and aggression
- how the two relate (remembering that aggression is **not** acceptable).

It is important to start to get the message across that, despite provocation and even if we are stressed, we still have a responsibility to behave in a socially acceptable way. Our behaviour can make a situation worse, inflame it or calm it.

But is it always a bad thing to get angry? Can it ever be a good thing?

Brainstorm

Good points/benefits	Bad points/costs
– gives us energy	– hurts others/self
– makes us deal with things	– lose friends/lonely
– provides a sense of control	– can't think or reason
– makes us brave enough to	– get into trouble
say something we wanted to	– feel awful

Discuss

Introduce

- the idea that although there are some things that would anger most people, for example having a personal possession stolen, often an event will not anger us all to the same degree, or even at all.
- Begin to collect more information on each individual's anger triggers and form a hierarchy of provocations. This can be kept in a client's folder and added to as triggers are discovered through self-monitoring and recordings. Novaco (1993–4) suggests using index cards to record anger experiences, and grading the degree of anger experienced. Clearly, clients will need help with this process, but these anger hierarchies can be used later when new skills are applied and practised in progressively more difficult situations (this is the application training stage of the stress inoculation treatment).

So we are beginning to learn that each of us may get angry because of different things. We are also going to keep records of our own anger triggers to help us understand our personal patterns of anger.

Now look at the hierarchies or brainstorming list from Session 1, and consider:

- Do these things always make you angry in the same way?
- What affects our anger?

Ask the group to suggest ideas, such as:

- *how we were when we woke up – grumpy?*
- *what else has gone wrong*
- *how noisy it is*
- *how well we slept*
- *who said that remark to us.*

Use examples to illustrate this idea.

But we can prevent some of these things, or at least be aware of them. Talk about adjusting the environment to avoid anger arousal.

Homework

Continue self-monitoring. Repeat the method used or adjust as necessary.

Relaxation/arousal reduction

Continue with calming breaths or step 1 of OTSAR (see Appendix 1). Promote their use:

- calming breaths are easy to use
- you don't need a relaxation mat or any special equipment
- they can be done anywhere, at any time.

Therapist's notes

Breathing and relaxation are a vital part of anger control. When we are angry or anxious our bodies pump out adrenaline. This, in turn, is likely to lead to fast, shallow breathing and alters the balance of oxygen and carbon dioxide circulating in the blood. If this imbalance is not corrected, it can stimulate further release of adrenaline and lead to even more anger or stress. Therefore, taking control of this snatched breathing by forcing a slower, deeper and regular pattern of breathing can hinder the effects of the excess adrenaline. The result should be an increased sense of calmness and control and, therefore, a greater chance of future behaviour being based on judgement, rather than on impulse.

Hence, breathing is a key part of 'On The Spot Arousal Reduction' or OTSAR. It is therefore the first step of OTSAR, the method of which will be gradually introduced along with self-statements as a quick technique to 'take the edge off' the level of arousal. It can complement full relaxation, or be an alternative, user-friendly, coping device (see Appendix 1 for information on OTSAR).

SESSION 4

Welcome

Check homework

- Did anyone do any self-monitoring?
- Give praise if they did, but remember it may take a while to establish the habit.

Feedback

Ask about each person's week, both the situations that ended well and those that were a problem (staff input may be useful here).

This process helps to:

- establish the normality of anger
- discourage denial of getting angry
- raise awareness of monitoring self
- establish some support/understanding within the group.

BUT BEWARE OF GLORIFICATION OF INCIDENTS AND ENSURE REPORTING IS NOT AN OPPORTUNITY TO CRITICISE OTHERS

Recap

- on previous theory of anger versus aggression
- the good and bad points of anger
- that things around us affect our anger.

We said that anger may lead us to **DO** different things (change our behaviour) but that is not the only way anger changes us.

> ANGER CHANGES THE WAY WE THINK, FEEL AND BEHAVE

Practical

This week we shall think about how it changes our bodies (the feeling part).

- Ask for a volunteer to lie on the floor on a large sheet of paper and draw around them. If this is not appropriate, provide a printed sheet such as the 'outline of a person' worksheet found in Appendix 1.
- Then divide into two small groups (with a member of staff in each) and brainstorm what happens to your body when you are angry, i.e. increased heart rate, change in colour, tense muscles, etc.
- Re-form into a large group to give feedback, and mark the changes on the paper body as they are mentioned.
- Discuss all the effects and how the poor old body suffers, e.g. headache, stiff neck, stomach ache, feeling sick, shaky, tired or having a tight chest.

> YOUR BODY DESERVES BETTER THAN THIS!

Homework

Continue with self-monitoring, but take notice of the 'feeling part'. Use the 'outline of a person' worksheet (Appendix 1) or a simple diary, as in Appendix 4.

Relaxation/arousal reduction

- Continue practising calming breaths – step 1 of OTSAR (Appendix 1).
- Now introduce step 2 of OTSAR, and allow longer for this procedure.
- Explain and demonstrate the difference between tense and relaxed postures.
- Then allow individuals to try them, using whichever position (sitting or lying down) is most acceptable to them.
- Give feedback on how they looked.
- Ask how they felt (proprioceptive feedback).

Therapist's notes

Tension is an early sign of anger arousal, and so if tension is high we are more easily provoked. Therefore, it is necessary to learn to recognise tension as a WARNING SIGN.

It is important that we are aware of the difference between tensed and relaxed muscles; this can be learned through relaxation training. Once we are able first to self-monitor and then differentiate between the two bodily states, we can choose to take a certain course of action as tension arises. If we are well rehearsed in this action it can be implemented even in quite challenging situations. Any extra relaxation sessions offered in addition to this work will enhance the effect.

Many clients who have acquired a brain injury report that they experience very intense and rapidly rising levels of arousal. They may be fearful of their potential loss of control, which in turn increases the level of anxiety arousal. With this group in particular, it is important to teach them ways of picking up the warning signs, arresting the arousal and adjusting their environment. All of this has to be done before any reasoning is carried out.

SESSION 5

Welcome

Check homework

Praise any recordings.

Feedback

Review any anger arousal since the last session. Look at situations that ended well and those that were a problem.

Ask questions such as:

- *what started it all?* (trigger)
- *what did you do?* (behaviour)
- *was anyone hurt?* (awareness)
- *how did it all end up?* (consequences)
- *did you lose out?* (consequences)
- *did you get into trouble?* (consequences)
- *did your body feel different?* (arousal)
- *was it worth getting angry?*

Recap

Being angry leads us to **think**, **feel** and **behave** differently.

- In the last session we were looking at the body changes (the feeling part). Reproduce the drawing of the body from the last session.

- Remind members of the changes in the body – of the effects on the body and on our health – if we are in a tense state too often, and for too long.

Practical

- Last session we took longer for relaxation and started to learn the difference between tense and relaxed muscles.
- We need to take notice of the tension and treat it as a **warning sign**.

Any ideas about what can we do to calm our body when we get that warning sign? Brainstorm ideas such as:

- take long deep breaths – get rid of the hot air
- push our shoulders down
- alter posture, e.g. if standing, sit down
- stretch out arms and legs and break the tension
- check fingers are opened out – no fists
- take a slow walk
- have a cool drink
- take gentle exercise, such as swimming.

Homework

Continue self-monitoring as before, so as to raise awareness of anger arousal.

Relaxation arousal/reduction

Allow longer for this, as in the last session.

Therapist's notes

People often feel that they must release the anger from their body by vigorous exercise, or by other substitute activities such as using a punch bag. However, caution should be exercised, for far from getting rid of the anger, these activities may maintain the levels of physiological arousal at a high level. So if the arousal following the vigorous activity is not reduced by calming-down exercises, it may well remain only to transfer to a provoking situation in the near future. This can explain why, at times, a minor annoyance can result in an experience of intense anger.

It is also clear that it is not just a case of getting it out of your system, for the thoughts or cognitions that originally fuelled the anger will remain there to do so again unless they are reappraised or challenged.

Therefore, if individuals wish to participate in vigorous exercise because they are angry, encourage them also to have a winding-down period afterwards. Try a slow walk with long stretching steps and the arms loosely swinging whilst the breathing returns to a gentle regular pace. This will allow the physiological arousal levels to decline before the individual may encounter another provocation. However, more importantly, encourage them to 'rethink' their anger to see if it was justified and, if so, to voice any grievances calmly.

SESSION

6

Welcome

Check homework

Praise any recording.

Feedback

Check on any anger arousal since the last session.

Recap

- We have been looking at the changes that can take place in our body when we get angry (use our drawing of the body as a prompt).
- *Has anyone felt any of these changes since the last session?*
- Use any discussion as revision.

SO ANGER CAN MAKE OUR BODIES FEEL DIFFERENT!

Introduce

- Describe the 'anger thermometer' (see Appendix 1).
- Explain the analogy of 'boiling up' or 'being cool' to anger and calm.
- Allow each person to relate their present 'feelings' (level of arousal) to the scale.

Discuss

Give an example of an angry situation.

- Do our feelings change?
- Do we go up the thermometer?

Role-play

- Therapist/therapist or therapist/client, role-play a typical situation that would be provoking to individuals.
- Refer to arousal levels on the thermometer.
- Discuss.

Homework

Continue with self-monitoring (a diary sheet that includes a picture of the thermometer may now be used, see Appendix 4).

Relaxation/arousal reduction

- Afterwards, look at the thermometer and rate levels of arousal.

Feeling calm before you leave?

Therapist's notes

The use of a visual aid such as the anger thermometer has proved helpful for individuals when learning to quantify their anger. Any fun measuring scale could be used.

Other suggestions are: a kettle (with a lid that blows off at boiling point), a bottle of fizzy pop with a top that could blow.

SESSION 7

Welcome

Check homework

Praise any recording.

Feedback

- Check on each person's week, situations that ended well, or not so well.
- Use the thermometer to measure levels of arousal.

Recap

On earlier sessions:

- the changes that take place in our bodies when we start to get angry
- refer to the drawing of the body
- how can we tell if it is happening?
- how might our bodies **FEEL** as we 'boil-up' or go up the thermometer?

Introduce

- the idea that as we get angry our thoughts also change. This concept is hard to grasp for many, so it is introduced in a general way rather than person-specific.

Discuss

- Explore what people may 'think' when they are angry.

- Use the bubble picture (see Appendix 2) to illustrate the thoughts of an angry person compared with those of a happy contented person.
- Describe two scenarios or role-play scenes around the above point, and discuss the possible resulting behaviours and physiological arousal.

Relaxation/arousal reduction

- Use the thermometer before and after.
- If clients have grasped the difference between tense and relaxed muscles and are beginning to self-monitor when asked to, then step 3 of OTSAR can be introduced.

Homework

- Continue using the thermometer diary and rate levels of arousal.
- Practise any of the above relaxation/arousal reduction techniques.

Therapist's notes

Feindler uses the term trigger to describe the anger-provoking event or antecedent. This could be a direct provocation (verbal, physical or gesture), or an indirect trigger which is associated with the individual's internal appraisal or perception of a situation. If these appraisals are distorted, unhelpful self-statements will be present (e.g. *they are late on purpose just to wind me up*). Current triggers that provoke anger can be linked to the person's past, as well as their expectations and beliefs. We all acquire a collection of 'old tapes' or cognitions that can be triggered by a current event; for example, being shouted at today could set off the 'old tapes' of when parents used to bully us in childhood.

The trigger may be misinterpreted if an individual's information processing is impaired. Having to struggle to extract the meaning of a situation may lead to anxiety, feeling stupid, loss of control, and anger, either at ourselves, or the need to place the blame externally.

SESSION

8

Therapist's notes

Moving on to the **skill acquisition** and **application training** phases:

It is expected that the assessment, interview, any pre-sessional work and the block of sessions so far, will have completed the **cognitive preparation** work. Therefore, it is hoped that the client will be:

- engaged in treatment
- aware of the costs of their anger
- working, with the therapist, to learn their own patterns of anger
- developing the fundamentals of self-monitoring
- appreciating the components of anger (physiological, behavioural and cognitive)
- interested in learning alternative ways of coping.

This now leads into the **skill training phase**. The **application of skills** is incorporated during this, and during any additional sessions (see page 107) plus follow-up sessions.

Welcome

Check homework

Feedback

Reviews on events since the last session.

- Was anyone aware of any changes in their body as they started to get angry?
- Was everyone practising their relaxation/arousal reduction techniques?

Recap

- When we get angry our **thoughts** change and that effects our **bodily feelings** and **behaviour**.

Practical

- Work in pairs and use the 'angry man' bubble picture (see Appendix 2). Write in examples of thoughts when angry.
- Staff input may be needed in each group.

People often feel that they shouldn't think bad thoughts and so it may be difficult for them to write them down.

Explain

Some thoughts, for example:

- *I want to hurt him*
- *it's not fair*
- *why are they doing this to me?*

are unhelpful and actually help to 'wind us up', whereas others, such as:

- *I must talk to someone and try to sort this out*

might not do so, for they are more helpful and constructive (some say they calm us and act as tranquillisers!).

- Look again at bubble pictures and spot which thoughts are 'wind-up thoughts', and which are not. Mark the unhelpful thoughts to distinguish them from any helpful calming thoughts.

- Use the hand-outs of 'wind-up' and 'helpful calming' thoughts (see Appendix 2).

NOTE: THIS ASPECT IS DIFFICULT TO GRASP AND WILL
         TAKE A GREAT DEAL OF REPEATED EXPLANATION.
         CONSEQUENTLY, MORE TIME IS GIVEN TO IT .

Homework

Use another bubble picture (see Appendix 2) to record some 'hot', angry thoughts during the week. Staff may need to help if individuals have poor literacy skills, or if they need tactful encouragement to remember incidents!

Relaxation/arousal reduction

Describe Step 3 of OTSAR, or your method of preference. Use the thermometer before and after to monitor any changes. We can wind ourselves up, so we must:

LEARN TO WIND DOWN!

Therapist's notes

Self-statements – the way we think – can affect how we feel in a fairly direct, intentional fashion. We can influence our thoughts by a sort of internal monologue – an ongoing series of statements to ourselves – in which we tell ourselves what to think and believe, and even how to behave (Meichenbaum 1985). These self-statements have a direct effect on physiological symptoms and the decision-making process.

This is the core ingredient of anger management.

SESSION

9

Welcome

Feedback

Review the week, **but don't look at the homework yet,** we shall use it during the session.

Recap

Recall last week's session.

- Remind ourselves what unhelpful wind-up thoughts are.
- Now look at the homework (decide if it is most appropriate for this to be done quietly with a staff member or in front of the group).
- *Is it becoming clear which are the unhelpful thoughts?*
- Use examples to demonstrate – *would thinking those 'wind-up' thoughts over and over again take you up the anger thermometer?*
- Contrast with a suitable calming, helpful thought and refer to the thermometer again. Examples of positive self-statements are in Appendix 2.

Role-play

- Choose a scene that is familiar to group members, where a person is repeatedly thinking 'wind-up' thoughts. The therapist could then role-play the scene whilst the rest of the group observe any effect on that person's body and behaviour.
- Afterwards, discuss the effect and draw attention to the key points.

| EVENT (trigger) | THINK $\longrightarrow$ FEEL $\longrightarrow$ DO $\longrightarrow$ |

The sequence above can be drawn on a whiteboard as a demonstration, but it is likely that individuals will be able to identify with either end before the middle!

- Again, make a contrast by repeating the scene when the person is thinking calm, peaceful thoughts.
- Refer to the thermometer.

So do we all experience wind-up thoughts?

Most people do, but are we aware of them?

- Use the Think → Feel → Do sequence hand-outs to illustrate the sequence (see Appendix 2).

The homework and the sessions should help us to learn to notice our 'wind-up' thoughts compared with more helpful calming ones.

Homework

Repeat of bubble pictures or other diaries.

Relaxation/arousal reduction

- Learning to 'wind down'.
- Step 3 of OTSAR.
- Check level on the thermometer afterwards.

Therapist's notes Understanding the cognitive aspects of anger arousal

So far we have established a very simplistic connection between thoughts, emotions (in this case anger) and behaviour. There is much more to the cognitive aspects of anger (explained more fully in Appendix 2), but at present the therapist needs to appreciate that the following influence anger arousal:

1. **Noticing the provocation** in the first place! Some people, more than others, are tuned to notice things that will annoy them. This could mean that their focus of attention shifts towards the potential provocation. This can be a reflection of their past experiences, for example people who have been exposed to confrontation or physical abuse in the past have a tendency to be 'on guard' against further abuse. For them, this may be an adaptive response because it prepares them for a situation that could be interpreted as potentially hurtful.
2. **Expectations** – unrealistic or rigid expectations can 'set us up' for anger. Some people expect trouble, or that the situation will end up in an argument/fight.
3. **Appraisal** – a situation may be perceived as a threat. This automatic process depends on past events (old tapes) as well as on rules and beliefs.
4. **'Wind-up' thoughts** – based on the above, can fuel the level of arousal.

So our interpretation of an incident, how we feel it will affect us, and what we say to ourselves all select and govern the emotion we feel.

How much of this aspect can be taught?

As much as the individuals can understand, but point 4 is the most important. Some individuals grasp very little of the cognitive aspects of anger and are able to follow only simple behavioural instructions, i.e. *breathe out, push your shoulders down and walk away!* This of course is a successful way of avoiding a confrontation, but it does not address levels of residual arousal or, more importantly, stop the 'wind-up' thoughts which may lead to future rumination and further arousal.

Sessions 15–18 will include further cognitive restructuring work for those clients who are able to grasp this aspect of treatment.

SESSION

10

Welcome

Check homework and feedback

Since the last session:

- were any angry thoughts recorded?
- did they fuel an angry situation?
- how was the week?

Recap

On the physiological and cognitive aspects of anger:

- the unhelpful wind-up thoughts
- any resulting changes in the body and behaviour

The THINK ⟶ FEEL ⟶ DO sequence

(T ⟶ F ⟶ D)

What might we do as a result of having these thoughts and getting wound up?

Practical

- Brainstorm what people do at present.
- Some examples may be helpful, e.g. listen to music, talk to others, etc., but some will be poor coping skills, e.g. getting wound-up, go up the thermometer, and then become aggressive!
- Naturally, reinforce the adaptive behaviours but also be reassuring and optimistic for those who 'lose it'.

Therapist's notes

By now it is hoped that individuals have some understanding about their anger, and will have acquired the confidence to acknowledge its presence.

Introduce the idea that each of us has a choice as to how we behave and has responsibility for our own actions. This can be a foreign concept for those who are dependent upon others and consequently may feel themselves to be 'a victim of the system'.

We all enjoy being able to attribute 'what has happened' to somebody, or something, else, for this makes us feel free of responsibility, and it is comfortable. However, these external attributions have to be challenged, without apportioning blame or guilt, to allow the individual to take ownership of their behaviour.

This is a way of empowering the individual.

Now suggest that we can learn better ways of coping when we feel that we are beginning to boil-up, or to sense the warning signs.

- Explain that thinking about your anger tends to make it worse, but how can you stop? Distraction can be helpful by not letting you pay any attention to your anger – but again, how?

Any ideas of things to **DO** *or* **THINK?**

- Work in pairs or singly, use the worksheet 'Ways To Calm' to record any suggestions that are offered (see Appendix 4). A completed version is also included for extra ideas.
- Share suggestions and pick out any that could be unhelpful. Reinforce the good ones!
- Keep the sheets, we shall repeat the exercise at a later date to see if there are more ideas.

Homework

Continue with simple diaries (pictorial, if literacy skills are poor). Encourage group members to prompt and support each other with the task.

Relaxation/arousal reduction

By now the technique of **O**n **T**he **S**pot **A**rousal **R**eduction must be coming familiar, and the discipline of 'turning it on' to demand, is hopefully being practised.

- In this session, before starting the procedure, encourage each person to get up and pace around while remembering an anger-provoking situation, then to find a chair 'plonk themselves in it' and commence the arousal reduction. This is still step 3 of OTSAR.
- Look at the anger thermometer and register the level of arousal before and after.

SESSIONS 11/12

Welcome

Check homework and feedback

Recap

Review the discussion about:

- what people **DO** when they are angry – remember some were helpful and others were not
- our having a choice and a responsibility for our behaviour
- the list of ideas of what to do or think when getting angry (produce the worksheet from the last session).

So what's going to make us do or think these things ?

Introduce

Self-Instruction Training – the 'think aloud' approach, or things that we say or think to ourselves to remind us to:

- do different actions e.g. *move away*
- reduce body arousal e.g. *breathe out, shoulders down*
- question our thoughts e.g. *maybe he didn't mean it*

This is about learning to follow certain steps to calm down!

But in the heat of an angry moment we may not remember the self-instruction and may need:

REMINDERS!

Show examples of visual prompts:

- a small pocket size card or
- pages to fit into a coping book
- posters on the bedroom wall may be useful.

Each contains instructions to:

- gain attention and stop automatic thoughts, e.g. *Stop Helen!*
- reduce arousal, e.g. *calm down, breathe out…*
- a distraction, e.g. a picture or a poem
- a prompt to say *well done!* if successful (a tick or a thumbs-up!)

Some may like THE TRAFFIC LIGHT ROUTINE (see Appendix 4) but please note this could upset those who have been involved in a road traffic accident.

The idea is that reading the message on the card will interrupt the 'wind-up thoughts' and provide instruction on what to do:

Because when I am angry I can't think of anything else apart from how angry I am!

The prompt card/book/message/picture should act as a firm instruction, 'The Bossy Book', – call it whatever is acceptable to the person concerned, make it a user-friendly gimmick!

Next week we shall make these visual prompts – cards, etc., so think of ideas of what to have on your 'coping card', and bring any pictures, messages, poems, funny postcards to the session.

Homework

Continue with the simple diaries.

Relaxation/arousal reduction

- Step 3 of OTSAR. Encourage each person to pace around remembering an angry situation, then to plonk themselves in a chair before starting the technique.
- Look at the anger thermometer and register the level of arousal before and after.

Therapist's notes

Feindler and Ecton (1986) describe how self-instruction has been used to train impulsive youngsters to provide themselves with internally generated verbal commands, or guiding statements. These help to inhibit an automatic aggressive response, and prompt a more adaptive one. She asserts that 'adolescents who exhibit impulsive aggression have clear deficits in self-guiding speech'.

The original work on self-instruction with impulsive 4-year-olds. (Meichenbaum and Goodman 1971) involved a sequence:

1. The therapist models the task performance and self-instructs out loud. In this case, statements such as: 'breathe out, put your hands in your pocket, and walk away', while the child observes.
2. The child performs the task, instructing himself out loud as he does so.
3. The therapist models the task performance and whispers self-instruction while the child observes.
4. The child repeats the above.
5. The therapist performs the task using covert self-instructions with pauses and behavioural signs of thinking, e.g. raising eyes towards the ceiling, touching his/her face, and so forth.
6. The child performs the task using covert self-instructions.

This sequence can be applied with individuals of any age if they require additional help in modelling and rehearsing the task.

SESSIONS 13/14

Welcome

Check homework and feedback

- Look at diaries.
- Use the thermometer to illustrate arousal levels described.

Recap

Last week:

- *we agreed that we all get unhelpful thoughts that can 'wind us up'*
- *we talked about how to interrupt or stop these by self-instruction*
- *we decided that prompt cards could be useful to use when we feel ourselves boiling up.*

Practical Session

Make the coping cards or visual prompts.

It is important that each person suggests what they would like on their prompt card, which should be personal, unique and owned by the person concerned.

Discuss with each person:

- the choice of format
- what is acceptable to them (street cred)
- help them to decide on an instruction that they would take notice of if someone else gave it to them. e.g. *STOP GILL, breathe out and walk away.*

Because anger management is about self-management we are going to learn to instruct ourselves.

- Work in small groups and make cards/books (it is a wise idea to make a copy of each person's card in case of their being lost, or laundered!)
- Re-introduce the idea of **role-play**. Therapists demonstrate how to use the card in a typically provocative situation, e.g.

Bill is sitting quietly in the lounge when along comes Fred looking for his lost cigarettes. Fred assumes that Bill must be sitting on them and tries to move Bill from the chair. Bill is annoyed and indignant, but manages to state that he is not sitting on them! Fred, however, is not interested in listening to any explanation, and an argument ensues.

- Repeat role-play but with Bill producing his card and following the prompt shown:

STOP BILL – KEEP CALM – BREATH AWAY THE ANGER!

- Discuss the difference in Bill's response and probable mood matching from Fred as a result. Was there any difference in resulting behaviours? For example, did Fred apologise?
- Allow other members to 'have a go' and then discuss their efforts and feelings on how it went.

Discuss

- WHEN to use the card.
- Re-cap on recognising the warning signs, otherwise learning when to use the coping skills will be difficult.
- By now it should be coming clear, to both the therapist and the participants, what are the likely triggers of anger.
- Various alternative scenarios can then be shown so as to demonstrate the use of the card.
- Explain that in time using the card will become a habit, and that later it may be enough just to think of the card, or tap it in the pocket, rather than producing it each time anger is felt.

Homework

1. Practise using the coping cards.
2. Continue to use diaries, if participants are still willing to do so. This helps to establish the particular patterns of anger, and also to monitor the severity and frequency (albeit from probably erratic recording) of the anger incidents.

Relaxation/arousal reduction

*   Use step 3 of OTSAR – but perhaps include some self-statements to coincide with any coping cards/books.
*   Look at the anger thermometer and register levels of arousal before and after.

Therapist's notes

Cognitive techniques will need to be modified for use with this group of patients. Altering interpretations, for example, requires advanced capabilities; nevertheless, the principles of **thought stopping** (Wolpe, 1973) and **self instruction** (Meichenbaum 1985) techniques can be applied. The former to interrupt the T $\rightarrow$ F $\rightarrow$ D $\rightarrow$ sequence, the latter to direct coping provision of a visual prompt that combines techniques may be necessary.

SESSIONS 15–18

Welcome

Feedback

- Look at diaries/bubbles or ask for oral feedback.

  - *Did anyone use their cards/books?*
  - *Were they useful?*

- If cards have been forgotten, lost or washed, be patient; it may take a while to establish the habit of using them. Some people do find it a strange thing to do, so encourage group members to support and prompt each other.

Note: If it is possible to pursue the cognitive restructuring work it will be necessary for the therapist to have some understanding of the important influence that cognitive therapy has had on work with anger problems.

The core of cognitive therapy is that our thoughts influence our mood, emotion, physical reaction and behaviour. So when teaching a client to manage their anger, the cognitive aspects are very important (see Therapist's notes overleaf).

Because of the difficulty that clients find with this abstract concept, therapists will no doubt have to tailor treatment delivery to their client group. Appendix 2 contains various exercises that have been devised to help explain that distorted cognitions set up individuals for anger.

It is expected that this stage may take a few sessions, say three or four, but, as already mentioned, if the therapist assesses that the client group cannot master the abstract concept continue to practise self-instruction training.

Therapist's notes

When a person is angry the thoughts that are flying through their head seem real, valid and justified, hence in turn they will maintain the anger arousal. On closer analysis the thoughts are often negative, distorted, and perhaps unrealistic. Burns (1990) refers to distorted or twisted thinking; here are some examples applied to anger.

All-or-nothing thinking
You see things in black-or-white categories. Things are either right or wrong. If something is not as planned then it is a total failure. So if your benefit book has not yet arrived at the post office when you go to collect it, your thinking might be: *It's all gone totally wrong – it is a disaster!*

Overgeneralisation
You see a single event as part of a regular pattern. You make sweeping statements, often using the words 'always' and 'never', for example if the bus is late you might think: *That's it, it's **always** late, I'm **never** going on a bus again.*

Mental Filter
You discount the positives and pick on a single negative detail, dwell on it, and this winds you up. So when your neighbour helps you with your chores but misses one out, you focus on that, thinking: *see, she couldn't even finish the job!*

Jumping to conclusions
You interpret things negatively even though there are no facts to support your conclusions. You guess what people are thinking (mind-reading) and then make up explanations for their behaviour; for example, one day you see your friend looking serious and rushing past, but because she does not speak to you, you think: *She hates me, so much for her friendship!*

Magnification (making a mountain out of a molehill!)
You exaggerate the importance of your problem and feel it is a catastrophe; so, for example, if the washing machine is not emptying, your thinking might be: *How awful, how terrible, I've got no clothes to wear, this is the end!*

Emotional reasoning
You take your emotion as evidence for the truth. So: *I feel angry; that proves that you must have been treating me badly.*

'Should' statements

Shoulds, oughts and musts' are said to be illogical rules! They are meant to motivate and give standards but they can be rigid and lead to guilt and disappointment when directed at yourself; or anger if directed at others. *I must never forget things*, or, *people should always be on time!*

Labelling

This is a form of all-or-nothing thinking. You are quick to give yourself or others a negative label, attacking the person rather than what they did. This highly charged language leads to hostility and anger. So after one human mistake has been made, accusations of:

I'm useless! or, *she's a lazy...., he's an excuse for a man!* might be said.

Personalisation or blame (attributional bias)

You hold yourself or others responsible for some external event that is out of your/their control. **I** *got angry because* **you** *messed up everything today!*

SESSIONS 19-21

Welcome

Feedback

- Look at diaries/bubbles or ask for oral feedback.

    - *Did anyone use their cards?*
    - *Were they useful?*

- Again, be patient if cards have been forgotten or lost. Remember, it may take a while to establish the habit of using them. Some people do find it a strange thing to do, so encourage group members to support and prompt each other.

So far we have concentrated on reducing levels of anger arousal by learning ways to keep the body and thoughts calm. We also need to learn new ways of explaining ourselves effectively if the anger is justified and something has to be said. Therefore, during this part of the skill acquisition phase it important to teach skill building, as well as arousal reduction techniques.

Introduce the Assertive way

- This is a good way of responding when we feel 'fired up'.
- Being assertive means saying clearly what we want, need and/or feel, whilst at the same time respecting the needs wishes and feelings of others.
- It is **not** about getting our own way or winning all the time.

- It is more about 'saying our piece' and consequently feeling that we have not let ourself down.
- We do not have to be aggressive in order to get our point across!
- We do not have to be passive, have no control, and 'feel like a doormat'. This can mean that we get anxious, or that we then get annoyed with ourselves because we couldn't say what we felt. Sometimes that anger builds up, and we end up 'overdoing it' and being aggressive! Then we feel guilty.
- Being assertive is OK, it is NOT selfish and it often leads to a better end result!
- It is assertive to say if we don't understand – *could you please tell me again, I didn't catch it all.*
- Emphasise that when we have the necessary skills we do have a choice.
- Use the **Signpost Handout – The Assertive Way** to illustrate that choice (see Appendix 3 for handout and more on assertion training).

Let's learn how to be Assertive

Non-verbal behaviour. How do I look?

- Look the person in the eye.
- Stand tall and hold up your head.
- Have an open posture, no threats.
- Respect the other person's space, DO NOT stand too close.
- Use gestures that are firm but NOT threatening, e.g. open hands facing down when saying NO!
- Look as if you mean what you say, i.e. the non-verbal behaviour needs to match the words you are saying.

Verbal content. What to say

- Know what you want to say – plan it.
- Say it! Give a short simple message.
- Stick to that message, repeat it if necessary.
- Speak firmly.
- Be clear and calm.
- Use self-instruction, e.g. keep it clear, stick to the complaint, don't start criticising him/her.

Do not
- shout
- swear
- stare
- get too close
- use threatening or rude gestures
- be sarcastic.

Role-play

Role-play situations that are reported as causing anger arousal. Choose some where the end result was good, and some where the end result was unfavourable to the person concerned.

As in Social Skills Training, follow the stages:
- dry run
- positive feedback (there is always something good you can say!)
- instruction and/or modelling using – assertion rather than aggression, coping cards and OTSAR
- re-run using the above – the practice stage
- further feedback.

To shape behaviour and allow a sense of mastery, comment on:
- non-verbal behaviours
- voice tone
- listening skills
- how the card could have been used.

Remember, assertion is linked to confidence!

We gain confidence from 'saying our piece' BUT we need confidence to say it, and the belief that we should say it!

Homework

1.   Practise using cards and arousal reduction when angry.
2.   Try to get into the habit of checking levels of arousal by thinking of the thermometer.

3.   Do this each morning, and if 'on the pink or red' use your breathing to calm down.

4.   Say 'well done' to yourself when it works!

Relaxation/arousal reduction

By now, individuals will be developing a preferred routine of the arousal reduction. This may include some distraction, thought stopping or imagery.

•   This session try out step 4 of OTSAR, the standing version.
•   Look at the thermometer before and after.

Therapist's notes

Use of video feedback.

There are many advantages to this, for it allows individuals to witness and evaluate their own behaviour before modifying it if necessary. Video can be a popular method of feedback, increasing the self-esteem and sense of participation. Yet be mindful of the individual's anxiety, for people do not learn well in a state of anxiety. When therapists participate in role-play it can be a source of amusement as well as a learning exercise for the group members. Also, use the video player to show excerpt from TV programmes (soaps) as examples of anger-provoking situations, and then discuss the response of the actors.

REMEMBER to gain the client's permission before using video recording.

SESSIONS 22–25

Welcome

Feedback

- From the week – look at diaries/bubble pictures or ask for oral feedback.
- Discover incidents that were handled well (remained in control) as well as those that were a problem.

Role-play

- Role-play any scenarios that presented difficulties. Do a dry run, feedback, consider alternative responses, re-run, etc.

Recap

On earlier sessions:

- We have talked about wind-up thoughts and more helpful thoughts.
- Some of these are on your coping cards.
- So far we have used the cards when we start to feel angry, but they can also be used at other times.

How to prepare for a potentially provoking situation

Often provocation occurs with very little warning but at other times we know that a potentially provoking situation is looming.

Brainstorm ideas of such situations, e.g.:

- Mental Health Review Tribunal
- meeting with an important official
- having to spend time with someone that you do not like
- watching a football match on TV with someone who supports the other team!

Some of these situations are VERY PROVOKING and others less so. Try to establish a hierarchy of provocations because when we practise preparing for the situations we shall start with the less provoking and work up to the VERY PROVOKING! Such situations can be prepared by using the:

Stress Inoculation Training – SIT

The principle is to train the individual to use self-instruction statements when approaching, confronting or leaving an angry situation. This should enable them to deal with that situation calmly. It works by encouraging:

a) Direct arousal reduction – *my muscles are getting tight – time to relax.*
b) Indirect arousal reduction through interrupting and challenging the thoughts *STOP -don't allow yourself to go up the thermometer, check the facts!*

See Appendix 2 for extra ideas of self-statements. The complexity of this technique can be graded, an example of a simplified, repetitive self-statement to reduce arousal and increase the feeling of control is demonstrated below.

In the exercise below the phrase '**get calm**' will be used as a prompt to carry out the quick 'on-the-spot' arousal reduction, or OTSAR, that we have been practising each week. Naturally, the wording can be adjusted to suit individuals' taste and choice, or it could be the same as that on the coping card. Try to ensure that this wording does not conflict with the message on the card.

Check

Make sure that everyone understands what is meant by **get calm**, practise when sitting, standing, queuing ...

NOW APPLY THIS TO A SITUATION – such as one of those suggested in the brainstorming exercise.

Write a list of prompts on the board.

1.   Prepare and reassure yourself before the situation – *Remember what you're trying to sort out and stick to that.*
2.   **Get calm** (deep breath, self instruction).
3.   Imagine how it might be. (They may lead to increased anger arousal.)
4.   **Get calm.**
5.   Think of the key points that you want to say – take responsibility if you are in the wrong.
6.   **Get calm.**
7.   Imagine what the other person is likely to say – and listen!
8.   **Get calm.**
9.   Say your piece – key points, then listen, don't argue back.
10.   **Get calm.**
11.   Resolve or accept the situation, it is not about winning, but it's about being assertive and feeling good with yourself, because at least you did your best!
12.   *Well done! I can only do my best*

Suggest that the client 'runs through' the procedure in their mind (or talks it through with the therapist) before they actually practise it.
       TRY THE TECHNIQUE OUT ON A SITUATION THAT IS ONLY A LITTLE PROVOKING and therefore have a good chance of success. Later on you can try it out in a more provoking situation, and so on.

Afterwards, congratulate yourself!

Homework

Practise using the new technique when there is a situation that is known to be potentially arousing.

Relaxation/arousal reduction

Step 4 of OTSAR – standing version.

Therapist's notes

In many instances, clients have deficits in planning which may present as difficulties with problem-solving. If such a difficult situation is accompanied by high levels of anger the individual may respond with an impulsive action. This is particularly the case with those who have suffered a brain injury. Clients have the difficult task of learning to:

a)   inhibit their automatic responses of anger and impulsivity, and

b)   plan and implement actions to cope with the situation.

Therefore, the above procedure complements the problem-solving routine that is introduced in the next session plan.

SESSIONS 26–29

Welcome

Feedback

Review any angry situations arising from the diaries. Discuss alternative ways of handling situations and role-play.

Introduce – The Problem Solving Routine

We often get angry if we come across what seems to be a problem to us. Problem-solving training can help here. Remember:

- Problems are common.
- We can't avoid them.
- Many can be resolved, through learning the technique.
- There is a routine to follow, don't be impulsive!
- When learning it, work in a group or with a therapist.

Therapist's Notes

A great deal has been written about the problem-solving approach based on the work of D'Zurilla and Goldfried (1971) and it has been used successfully with children, adolescents and adults. To most of us, problem-solving is so routine that we are unaware of the cognitive operations that we follow. But to some individuals, the inability to first recognise the situation as a problem that can be solved, and then solve it, can lead to anger. Hence, problem-solving is one of the components of the skill acquisition phase of anger management.

The Problem-Solving Routine

Ask yourself the following questions: –

1.   What am I concerned about?
        (identify the problem – is it fact or fiction?)

2.   What do I want to happen?
        (select a realistic goal)

3.   What can I do?
        (think of alternatives, generate a few)

4.   What will happen if I?
        (consider consequences, positive and negative, short and long term, i.e. feel better or two minutes but get into trouble big time in the long term!)

5.   What is my decision?
        (make a decision)

6.   Now do it!
        (implementation)

7.   How did it work?
        (evaluate, was it successful? Would you do it again? If not, would your second choice have worked?

This can look lengthy but after a while we learn to weigh up the pros and cons automatically. This worksheet is in Appendix 3.

Practical

- Decide on some problem situations and practise using the routine
- It is advisable to learn the routine when in a calm state because when arousal levels are down, judgement is up!
- Later, put this routine into action when angry. In this case an opening self-instruction might be: *OK it's not an awful mess, just a problem to solve*.

Homework

- Practise using the problem-solving routine, it might be a good idea to get someone else to do it with you until you are familiar with it.
- As always, begin the practice with problems that are reasonably easy to solve, not an insurmoutable one!

Relaxation/arousal reduction

Continue practising whichever method is popular.

Therapist's notes

It is hoped that by now individuals should have acquired some of the skills necessary to help them manage their anger. However, therapists should not assume that skills learned will generalise to the 'real world'. Imagery and behavioural rehearsal, role-play, modelling and graduated *in vivo* practice, all contribute to generalisation. The SIT and problem-solving routine both allow the use of all of these techniques.

SESSION 30

Welcome

Feedback

- *How's the week been?*
- *Did anyone need to use the problem-solving routine?*

Look at examples of situations (from diaries or feedback) when anger was:

- handled well and the individual kept control – encourage them to give themselves a pat on the back, they were in charge!
- anger arousal was up, and things did not end up so well.

Look what happened in problem scenarios, draw attention to the cost of that scenario, e.g.:

- lost privileges
- feeling upset
- brooding (ruminating)
- losing friends.

Now prompt the individual to ask the question, *did my anger help me in the situation?* and if their answer is NO then get them to think again!

Discuss alternative ways of reacting – show how the use of:

- assertion

- problem-solving
- calming self-statements

may have been helpful. Role-play such situations.

Homework

Practise the range of skills learned. Offer suggestions as to the type of situations to tackle, thereby helping the client to grade the application of skill and assisting them not inadvertently to set themselves up to fail!

Relaxation/arousal reduction

Continue practising whichever method is popular.

Therapist's notes addressing all aspects of the anger

What we **do** when we are angry is very important, particularly to those other people around us! If we are able to walk away from a situation without getting into a row, that is an adaptive way of coping. But is it a complete answer? The person who is walking away with a high level of physiological arousal and racing wind-up thoughts would probably say no!

So beware, the behaviour is only part of it. What about the level of arousal that the person is still left with? If it is not dealt with, the potential for another flare-up of anger is a strong possibility. Such a flare-up could occur as a result of a future trigger and one that could seem a small thing to deserve such a disproportionate amount of anger. So it is important to tackle all three components of the anger. The physiological arousal must be reduced as well the cognitions challenged and reappraised. Put in context, this means that removing yourself from a potentially angry situation is good –

BUT REMEMBER OTSAR!

ADDITIONAL SESSIONS (OPTIONAL EXTRAS)

ADDITIONAL SESSION

1

HOW TO COPE WITH BEING TOLD NO!

Discuss

- Does this happen to everyone at some time or another?
- It is just a part of life?
- Suggest some common situations.

Do we like to be told NO?
What is the effect on us?

Situations

You have a request, and despite an assertive explanation, reasoning, etc. the answer is NO!

Examples:

- a trip to town
- going to the canteen
- a home visit
- you want to get to your room for some peace, but it is locked, the nurse is on the phone, and can't listen, he/she indicates *come back later*
- you want to speak to your case manager, or social worker, but you are told that he/she is busy all day

What to do

Take notice of the warning signs

Self-monitor any change in:

–   body arousal (up the thermometer)
–   thoughts (wind-up thoughts)
–   voice getting louder.

Take action

–   Use self-instruction – remember your card if you have one.
–   Use thought stopping – *Stop Helen.*
–   Breathe away the anger – take two deep breaths.
–   Walk away from the situation.
–   Use calming thoughts:

   Oh well, let's hope I can go next week.
   Maybe it's not their fault.

–   Use distraction that demands concentration,
       e.g. count backwards from 100 or 10.
–   Look at a picture on your card.
–   Imagine your peaceful spot, i.e. that scene of a hill in Ireland !

Role-play

–   a situation that has caused a group member difficulty in the past.

Include OTSAR, self-instruction or thinking of the coping card, before following the instructions.

Praise if it works !

ADDITIONAL SESSION 2

DEALING WITH TEASING AND PROVOCATION

Discuss

Why people tease:

- *Is it to get a response or to get others into trouble?*
- *Do you ever tease others?*
- *How do you feel when you are teased?*

Brainstorm

How does being teased affect your:

- thoughts (cognition)
- feelings (arousal)
- behaviour (what do you do? Do you ever react?).

What are the consequences of your behaviour?

What to do

Take notice of the warning signs

Self-monitor any

- wind-up thoughts
- body tension, etc.

Take action

−   Use self-instruction and card if used.
−   Use thought stopping − STOP HELEN, THINK THIS THROUGH.
−   Breathe away the anger, take two deep breaths.

This is to 'KEEP A LID ON' your arousal whilst you consider the best way to react. Try to think of a way that will not allow the situation to blow up, yet not leave you feeling that the other person has got the better of you.

Choices

Use problem-solving methods to decide which of the following to use:

−   Ignore the person − remember people tease to get results, if you give a response, they have won! don't provoke or tease in return.
−   Leave, walk away.
−   Make a joke!
−   Agree with the teasing.
−   Imagine them wearing a funny hat or silly costume.

KEEP COOL AND BE PLEASED WITH YOURSELF!

Some of these are not easy to do, but tell yourself that *It will be worth it* and remember, if you don't react badly you will have got the better of them!

Role-play

−   situations that were mentioned in the discussion at the beginning of the session.
−   Use the problem-solving process to make a choice of which course of action to take.

Praise if it works !

ADDITIONAL SESSION 3

COPING WITH CRITICISM

Discuss

- Why we might be criticised?
- *Has anyone been criticised recently?*
- Make a list of examples.

Brainstorm

How does being criticised affect your :

- thoughts
- feelings
- behaviour – how do you react?

Do a cost/benefit analysis for each reported behaviour and then divide the behaviours into those that seem to make matters worse and do not pay-off, versus more appropriate responses. For example:

– argue back	OR	– speak politely
– swear		– don't swear
– run off		– stay and listen
– aggressive tone		– assertive tone
– ignore and look away showing no interest at all		– listen to the other person's point of view
– rude non-verbals signs		then they may listen
– no rude gesture		to yours
– sarcasm		– no clever comments
– laugh at the other person		– listen to their point

There may be a difference in your reaction depending upon whether the criticism is justified or not, i.e. fair or unfair.

What to do

Either way,

–   Listen, and check that you understand what was said.
–   Look at the other person.
–   Remember the thermometer, monitor levels.
–   Use self-instruction and arousal reduction.
–   Congratulate yourself if you stay cool!
–   Take time to decide if the criticism is justified or not.

If justified

–   Agree, admit to your mistakes (be assertive).
–   Explain your reason if you wish, (but NOT lengthy excuses).
–   Apologise if necessary.

If unjustified

–   Politely, but firmly disagree.
–   Give an explanation, if there is another reason.
–   Ask what makes them think that.
–   Express how you felt – upset, etc.

Practical

To role-play either giving or receiving criticism can be awkward for both parties. Therefore, it is advisable to ease into this technique by first using other exercises such as:

•   a discussion when people have opposing views on cars, smoking, football teams, music, etc. Allow participants to participate in this, or watch a pre-recorded video of people doing this. Here, criticism is aimed at the person's views rather than at the person themselves. Discuss the necessity to respect others' views and the importance of not taking things personally.

•   watching a pre-recorded video of staff being criticised, use examples when good and poor responses are shown, then discuss.

- As individuals watch the recording and observe the scene without being on the receiving end of the anger, it should be easier for them to make an objective observation. They should then be encouraged to use their problem-solving skills. Then it should be easier to make a rational choice about the response taken.

Role-play

Role-play situations that were mentioned at the beginning of the session e.g.

- You're late.
- You're untidy.
- You don't do your fair share of the chores.
- Your work is not good enough.
- Your flat/house is untidy and the care worker has just been to visit and suggests you clean it up!

- The empty chair technique can be used if people initially find it difficult or confusing to criticise other group members during role-play.

ADDITIONAL SESSION 4

BEING ON THE RECEIVING END OF ANGER

Discuss

–   what this might mean.
–   It could be someone 'sounding off' about others or feeling angry with you.
–   *Have we all been in this position?*

Brainstorm

How did this affect our:

–   thoughts?
–   feelings?
–   behaviour?

A person on the receiving end of anger, or just witnessing the behaviour of an angry person, can experience a great range of 'hot cognitions'. These will depend upon that person's 'old tapes' (past experiences, memories and expectations) and on whom the target of the anger is directed. It is common for individuals to experience fear, a need for revenge, worry or insecurity and, in turn, they may respond with attack, defence or avoidance. Anyone with a history of abuse may readily perceive the anger to be directed at them, even if it is not.

Look at the costs and the benefits of each of the behavioural responses that individuals report. What were the consequences? Did they make the situation better or worse?

What to do

–   Listen and try to understand what the person is actually angry about.
–   Give the angry person space.
–   Breathe slowly.
–   Think clearly.
–   Remain calm – tone of voice.
–   No sudden movements or large gestures (these can be perceived as threatening).
–   Use self-statements to keep yourself calm.

For example:

Sometimes I've been this angry, it will pass.
He/she must really be unhappy to be acting like this.
I'm not going to let him/her get to me.
He/she would like me to get angry too – but I'm not going to!
I'll get out now and talk to him/her later.
It's a real shame he/she's that upset.
Don't discuss it like this, we'll both say things we don't mean.

–   Try to see it from their point of view before you decide if you agree or disagree with their annoyance.
–   When you are both ready to talk more calmly, sit down and continue as above.
–   Don't take all that is said personally, but if you made a mistake be brave enough to admit it!
–   This does not mean that you always do everything wrong!
–   Apologise if you are at fault.
–   Ask if there is anything you can do to make the person feel better.

Role-play

Role-play situations that were mentioned in the initial discussion (the therapist may have to take the role of the angry person). Discuss the result, feeling of control and the use of self-statements.

ADDITIONAL SESSION

5

CARRYING A GRUDGE

Discuss

What we mean by this.
- *Have we ever done it?*
- *Is it worse with certain people?*
- *Does it last for a long time?*

Situations

For example:

- You have been upset by another client spreading rumours about you, teasing, or name calling, but you have to live in the same hostel/ward as them!
- Your neighbour told the warden that you have broken the rules by entertaining people of the opposite sex after hours.
- You have been lied to or let down.

Brainstorm

- *What will happen when you see that person?*
- *Will your level of arousal change (go up on the thermometer)?*
- *Will there be any warning signs?*
  such as changes to your:

    - body
    - thoughts
    - behaviour.

What do you do?

–   get revenge?
–   throw something?
–   take it out on someone else?
–   self-harm?
–   or what?

Do a cost/benefit analysis for each suggestion.

What are the alternatives?

It depends if you feel you must assert your feelings about the grudge. If so:

- Be firm but CALM when you tell the other person that you do not like what they are doing, and please will they stop it. Such assertion can give a sense of power and increased self-esteem.
- But remember that there is a chance you could risk escalating the arousal of the other person!

Or if you are able to keep a low profile and not let the comments get to you:

- Why should you let that person wind you up?
- You deserve better!
- Do your OTSAR!

However, when circumstances force you to be together:

Remember

Use self-statements to prompt the use of:

–   arousal reduction
–   your card if you have one.

Do this

- when you know you will be seeing them
- whilst you are in their company
- to reduce your arousal if it starts to increase
- when you have managed not to BLOW-IT!
- Congratulate yourself if the end result is better than usual.

Role-play

Role-play situations such as

- being shut in a lift with another person with whom you always row
- trying to watch the TV when people are nattering and bothering you
- being pestered by another client for cigarettes, money, etc.
- having to work alongside 'that person' who now goes out with your girl/boyfriend.

RECAP SESSIONS

Welcome/feedback

These sessions aim to recap what has been learnt over the past weeks.

Key points

Recognising the signs of anger: *What are they?* Brainstorm:

- signs of physiological arousal
- changes in cognition
- behavioural changes.

What do we do when we feel the warning signs?

Give each person an opportunity to reuse the worksheet 'Ways To Calm' (Appendix 4) and then say what they do when they are beginning to feel angry and how they cope. Compare the suggestions offered when the worksheet was used before (session 10). Summarise key points, i.e.:

- take action, take charge of the anger
- use the coping card/book
- long slow outward breath followed by two complete deep breaths
- count backwards, etc.

Once the instinctive response is arrested, leave it for the moment, calm down and decide what to do next, e.g.:

- Let it drop – maybe there is another side to it.

- Be assertive – if a point has to be made.
- Solve the problem (with help?).
- Think it through with someone, maybe have a quick grumble, but then try to see it from all sides.
- Humour!

Whichever method you use, if it works be pleased that you felt calm and 'kept a lid on' your anger! . . . . . WELL DONE!

Remember other ways of preventing stress and anger

Explain the importance of preventing stress and anger by adjusting lifestyle and habits and the importance of leisure activities, e.g.:

- purposeful use of time leading to satisfaction with our own efforts
- setting some time aside each day to do something enjoyable (your quality time)
- niggles and frustrations do not seem so bad if balanced with pleasurable activities
- self-esteem and mood are very closely linked to anger
- sleeping regularly
- eating a balanced diet
- getting some fresh air every day.

Therapist's notes

Learning to manage our anger is a complex task involving many components. Consequently this manual has touched on a number of training techniques, some of which will be more useful than others to any one person. It is hoped that the client has now built up a picture of his/her patterns of anger and of his/her preferred ways of coping. It is likely that in the past they will have been given conflicting advice of what to **do** when they are angry, rather than developing an understanding of, and then devising customised ways of coping with, their anger.

Designing a 'blueprint'

It may be helpful to issue each client with a copy of their own key points that they have to remember. They can form an individualised summary (often called a blueprint in cognitive therapy). Each client can then keep their special blueprint in their anger management file. The purpose is to:

a)   re-affirm their newly acquired skills

b)   have a written record for the benefit of the client and others involved in their care.

See example opposite.

Finish

Encourage participants to help and remind each other to use their new skills in Anger Management and, of course, Relaxation!

SUMMARY OF MY ANGER MANAGEMENT WORK

Name.   Fred . . . .   Date . . . .

My anger can cause me a lot of trouble and grief because:
sometimes I hit others, have lost friends, am not allowed out on my own, I don't like to feel out of control.

The warning signs are:

a sudden rush of strength in my body, heart beats faster, fists clench, I stare at the other person, nasty thoughts.

I know that on some days I am not as tolerant if:

I'm hot, tired, had bad thoughts in the night, or have been worrying.

My anger triggers are:

- *people looking at me (I can think they are a threat)*
- *people not understanding me*
- *getting blamed*
- *people watching me work*
- *being made fun of*
- *I often 'get the wrong end of the stick'.*

I have learned the following techniques to use:

- *regularly monitor how I feel*
- *try to start off the day calm*

- *go for a walk if I'm over 30 on the thermometer*
- *use my coping book when I start to feel angry*
- *breathing techniques – '3 in and 4 out'*
- *leave, think it through, and decide if it's worth a disagreement.*

My danger zone starts at number .... 60........
I must use my coping skills before I get near to that number(30+).

If I can't manage to take charge of my anger I need to:
Tell my carer (give him the quick signal) then go off have a quick run/fast walk, then slow down and focus on my coping book – well done!

BRINGING THE TECHNIQUES OUT OF THE TREATMENT ROOM

We cannot just deliver the treatment and hope that generalisation of skills will happen naturally. Therefore, we cannot assume that a behaviour acquired in the therapy session will carry over to other situations. Plans have to be made to ensure the transfer of skills, including tailoring the process to suit the needs of the individual. Feindler and Ecton (1986) speak of 'canned procedures' and stress that therapists must not deliver treatment verbatim.

Firstly, we have to cater for individual needs, such as modifying the speed of delivery, using specific training techniques, memory aids, etc.; and secondly we have to be mindful of the environmental triggers in the client's world. Both of these factors can affect the success of generalisation of skills. There are a variety of useful techniques that have been evaluated and incorporated into clinical practice (Goldstein and Keller 1987). Some of these can be implemented in the recap sessions, for example:

- overlearning a particularly difficult skill such as ignoring baiting from others – practise and praise success heartily!
- fading of prompts from others or from self. By this stage many clients find that they do not need to get their coping card out and look at it; instead, a gentle tap of their pocket will act as a reassuring prompt.
- self-reinforcement, or planning a regular treat for yourself if there has been a trouble-free period. Decide how this is to be evaluated and by whom, i.e. will it be up to the client to record or will they be dependent upon feedback from others? Ensure that the goals are achievable and that the frequency of the treats is such that they are worth working for!

- expecting that when clients try out new skills outside the treatment room the response of others cannot be guaranteed. At the end of treatment it is advisable to role-play what the client can self-instruct if the person on the receiving end is discouraging, or even irrational!

Other methods to assist generalisation of skills

In vivo practice for homework

- Set clear goals to achieve (small achievable realistic steps).
- Think it through before actually attempting the step.
- Prepare a coping routine that is usable by the person, i.e. self-instructions, arousal reduction techniques, distraction.
- How to remember it? reminders, prompt cards . . . .
- Rehearse using imagery or role-play.
- Self-monitor before completing the task.
- Now put into practice.
- Ensure arousal is DOWN before leaving the situation.
- Evaluate:

  - reward the positives
  - shape behaviour
  - be encouraging!

Follow-up sessions

Follow-up sessions, delivered on a less regular basis than the main course of treatment, have shown to be a productive way of retaining some support, yet withdrawing structure and prompts. Fading the frequency of the sessions avoids a sudden ending of the treatment and clients are not able to join the 'been there, done that – now I can forget it' frame of mind! Follow-up sessions act as a 'top up' or booster for all the hard work that has been carried out. Clients can be given reinforcement for the times that they coped well with their anger, and learn further about difficulties they may have encountered. Any unforeseen problems that may have occurred can be examined, coping styles identified and their implementation prepared for.

The importance of data collection, from whichever source is practical, completes the monitoring of progress (see page 42).

APPENDIX

APPENDIX 1

THE PHYSIOLOGICAL COMPONENT

RELAXATION AND AROUSAL REDUCTION

Increased physiological activity and muscular tension are often early signs of anger arousal. They usually occur before any behavioural action is taken. In the early stages of anger management treatment individuals may not be aware of these physiological warning signs. Therefore, it is necessary that they have education about the benefits of relaxation and an opportunity to develop awareness of tension areas. Only then can the individual learn to induce a relaxation response that is a crucial part of anger management.

If the physiological arousal can be arrested or reduced this should, in turn, reduce the likelihood of any impulsive and problematic behaviour being triggered. Being able to 'calm down' on cue happens only after a great deal of dedicated training and practice. Yet this is what we are aiming for in anger management. Some clients may already be familiar with, and practising, the techniques on a regular basis; this of course will be a great advantage to them. Yet many clients are resistant to relaxation for a variety of reasons because they:

- have tried it unsuccessfully
- can't see its relevance to managing anger, it is too passive to use in those heated moments
- have not been able to appreciate the difference between tense and relaxed
- hate lying down, feel vulnerable with their eyes closed
- have time to ruminate, which in turn increases arousal.

So when introducing relaxation as part of the anger management sessions there is a need to be creative, to 'sell it's benefits', even relabel it!

There are a variety of relaxation methods, all of which have their own theoretical backgrounds and a great deal written about them, including a thorough review by Payne (1995). When therapists teach relaxation techniques it is often their personal choice and experience that dictate which methods they use with clients. Nevertheless, ideally the therapist will be familiar with, and able to offer, alternative methods if a client has difficulty with the particular technique being used.

All methods of relaxation aim to reduce physiological arousal within the body. As this arousal is governed by the autonomic nervous system it is worth reminding ourselves of its role. The action of the *autonomic nervous system* is involuntary and designed to enable us to survive. It has two branches:

The sympathetic nervous system:

which prepares the internal organs for emergencies by producing changes known as the 'fight-flight' response. So when a person is, or perceives themselves to be, under threat, this system increases the activity of the heart and sends blood away from the internal organs to the voluntary muscles so that they are ready for action.

The parasympathetic nervous system:

which restores the body to a resting state in the absence of challenge, anger, fear or excitement as the parasympathetic system takes control. Yet we know that slowed breathing is also associated with parasympathetic activity. So by making efforts to slow down the breathing rate it may be possible to counteract the effects of the sympathetic nervous system and arrest the symptoms of arousal. The relaxation response (Benson 1985) is an example of this. Hence the breath *out* is an important part of slowing down the symptoms of arousal, and many breathing techniques include a longer breath out than in e.g. *breathe in for the count of 4, and out for the count of 6*. OTSAR is based on this theoretical concept and therefore always begins with a BREATH OUT (see next page).

OTSAR or ON THE SPOT AROUSAL REDUCTION

O n

T he

S pot

A rousal

R eduction

WHAT IS OTSAR?

- It is a way of reducing levels of physiological arousal.
- It is a method that can be graded and therefore easily used anywhere, anytime.
- It has the potential to be customised to suit an individual's needs.

OTSAR combines a number of techniques:

- breathing – this is a key point
- simple relaxation
- self-monitoring levels of arousal and measuring them by equating to a visual measure, e.g. the anger thermometer
- thought stopping
- distraction techniques
- calming statements – what to do, feel or think.

Breathing

Start with breathing out – breathe away the anger! Often people are told to 'take a deep breath' but this is not always a comfortable action to take at times of escalating anger and when breathing is becoming increasingly shallow. To take in a deep breath at this point can give the feeling of bursting! So BREATHE OUT first, before taking two complete deep breaths.

OTSAR is introduced in steps:

1.   calming breaths
2.   learning to self-monitor and differentiate between tense and relax
3.   chair version – work progressively through the body
4.   standing version
5.   learning to turn it on/off anywhere, anytime!

OTSAR CAN HELP YOU TO

- Avoid getting really angry by short-circuiting anger arousal before it becomes too strong (because once we are 'up on the thermometer' it is really difficult to interrupt the escalation).
- Take a cool look at the situation, put it into context.
- Think clearly, decide what to do, ask for help if necessary.
- Use the anger productively to get something done, get confidence to use assertion.
- Build up a better track record.
- Feel calmer, and this helps our general health and stress levels.
- Remember, the more angry you are the worse decisions you make!

WHEN TO USE IT

- when you feel the warning signs
- when you know you are entering a situation that will probably annoy you
- before being assertive
- when the 'wind-up thoughts' begin to race
- when you realise that your voice is getting louder.

HOW TO LEARN OTSAR

- step-by-step, starting with calming breaths. Please read on!

Step 1 of OTSAR – CALMING BREATHS

The first step of relaxation and arousal reduction is to become aware of the way we breathe, and to learn to look upon calming breaths as something that will help 'keep a lid on' the level of anger arousal.

Ideally these techniques should be learned whilst lying down, but if this is not popular, sit up straight in a chair. The therapist should first model how to take a deep breath properly, and then allow the individual to rehearse the technique.

Exercise

- Place one hand on your abdomen just above your waistline, and put the other on your chest.
- Breathe in your usual way and notice which hand rises when you take a breath in.
- *Was it the one on your chest or on your abdomen?* Most likely it was your chest and, if so, that means that you are breathing from your chest and using only the top space in your lungs (explain anatomy if appropriate). This happens more when you are angry or anxious and then it becomes more difficult to breathe properly.
- So the plan is to breathe so that the hand on your abdomen moves, and then we know you are filling the bottom part of your lungs, and breathing from your diaphragm.
- Take a long slow breath OUT and empty your lungs, then slowly breathe in and pull the air right down to the lower part of your lungs (your abdomen should rise, NOT your chest area), then as you continue to breathe in slowly bring the air up to your chest area. Hold for the count of 2 initially (later try for longer) then BLOW the air out through your mouth in one long slow breath.
- This may take time to practise.
- Later, the blowing out may be accompanied by a calming word, or a prompt from the coping card that is introduced in sessions 11/12.
- Once the technique of using the whole space in the lungs has been mastered, it can be used not only when the individual is lying down, but sitting, or standing. With practice, the technique can be carried out quite discreetly.

Step 2 of OTSAR – SELF-MONITOR/TENSE/RELAX

The second step means learning to self-monitor and differentiate between tense and relaxed muscles. This step can be achieved by following the principles of the well-known methods of relaxation that are listed below. It is not possible to describe all of these and, as explained earlier on page 17, many therapists are experienced in relaxation training and have determined which method is most suitable for their clients. However, if not, here is a list of recommended methods that can allow the individual to learn the difference between being tense and relaxed.

Jacobson (1938)

Progressive relaxation which aims to recognise tension in the body and then to relax.

Mitchell (1977)

Simple physiological relaxation – the procedure is to reposition joints and train the body to receive messages of comfort in a relaxed position.

Benson (1976)

The relaxation response based on meditative principles. It uses a simple repetitive mental device (word) to maintain attention.

Behavioural relaxation training (Schilling and Poppen 1983, Lindsay and Baty 1986a or b, Poppen 1989)

Observable states of relaxation learned through observation and imitation.

TIP: The key areas of the body to work on when angry are the:

- hands – no fists
- shoulders
- neck
- jaw

REMEMBER: at the end of any relaxation or OTSAR allow time to come out of the relaxing state gently:

- *Be aware of the sounds around you.*

- *Wiggle your fingers and toes.*
- *Open your eyes when you are ready.*
- *How do you feel? Where are you on the thermometer/scale?*

Step 3 of OTSAR – SITTING VERSION

Use when angry or practise each day anyway.

- Find a chair and 'plonk yourself' down. Sit well back into the chair and rest your arms on your thighs, or, on the arms of the chair.
- Spread your fingers apart and stretch them out. Now stop stretching.
- Breathe OUT – blow away the anger.
- Breathe in through your nose and out through your mouth, do this twice.
- Now take smaller breaths (or you will see stars) and concentrate on settling your body.
- Put both feet firmly on the ground so that they are well supported.
- Be aware of the chair under your legs and of supporting your back.
- Allow yourself to sink into the chair.
- Push your shoulders down towards your feet, then stop pushing, if they jump back up towards your ears, then repeat this.
- Remember your breathing – in through your nose and out through your mouth.
- Allow your eyes to close gently and now let's settle your head.
- Allow it to roll very gently first to one side and then to the other.
- Now let it find a comfy spot for your head to settle.
- Open your mouth slightly and wiggle your bottom jaw. Now close your lips but *not* your teeth. Swallow and rest your tongue on the bottom of your mouth.
- Allow the lines and frowns to go from your face, to smooth away, up and over the top of your head.
- Remember your breathing – in through your nose and out through your mouth.
- Think of your calming statement, your prompt card or coping book. (use this line only after session 11 when self-instruction is introduced)

- Monitor your level of arousal – think of the thermometer.
- If you feel more calm and less angry and tense –

BE PLEASED WITH YOURSELF!
WELL DONE!!

- Continue to breathe in peace and relaxation, and to breathe out the anger and tension.

Step 4 of OTSAR – STANDING VERSION

Use when you start to feel the 'warning signs' of anger or tension. It is also a good idea to practise this daily whether you feel angry or not.

- Breathe OUT – blow away the anger.
- Breathe in through your nose.
- Breathe out, push your shoulders down and stretch out your fingers.
- Breathe in through your nose.
- Breathe out and *stop* the stretching – allow your shoulders and arms to relax.
- Change your posture – move your feet and stretch up and back slightly – then *stop* and relax.
- Remember the steady breathing – in through your nose and out through your mouth.
- Make sure your shoulders are down and that your arms are hanging loosely by your side.
- Open your mouth slightly and wiggle your bottom jaw. Now close your lips but *not* your teeth. Swallow and rest your tongue on the bottom of your mouth.
- Screw up your forehead, then relax – allow the lines to go from your face.
- Think of your:

  - calming statement
  - that scene of relaxation.

- Concentrate on something in the room.
- Focus.
- Breathe regularly.
- Monitor your level of arousal – think of the anger thermometer.
- If you feel more calm, and less angry and tense:

BE PLEASED WITH YOURSELF!
WELL DONE!
YOU KEPT A LID ON THINGS!

Step 5 of OTSAR – LEARNING TO TURN IT ON/OFF ANYWHERE, ANYTIME

The final stage of OTSAR is to apply the techniques 'on the spot' anywhere, anytime. It is a routine that can be used whenever there are warning signs of anger. It should include:

- breathing OUT
- addressing body tension in key areas – hands/fists, shoulders, neck, jaw.
- thought stopping and/or distraction
- calming statements.

With practice this quick technique becomes a shortened and unobtrusive relaxation response. At a psychological level it is associating specific thoughts with a specific physiological state of reducing arousal. So in time and with practice the verbalising of relaxation self-statements should evoke the response.

CUSTOMISING OTSAR

The scripts for step 3, 4 and 5 can be customised for clients' individual needs and personal taste. The script can be recorded on a tape and issued to the client for use in their own time.

Note: keep a master copy of the tape – it could get lost!

An example of a customised version of step 3

This individual had worked through the course and was able to use imagery and self-statements. He also:

- wore glasses
- could not breathe through his nose
- had a 'special' picture that made him feel calm.

Script – use when angry, but also practise each day.

- Find a chair and 'plonk yourself' down. Sit well back into the chair and rest your arms on your thighs, or on the arms of the chair.
- Take off your glasses.

- Spread your fingers apart and stretch them out. Now stop stretching.
- Breathe OUT – blow away the anger – think of your coping card.
- Breathe in and out through your mouth, do this twice.
- Now take smaller breaths (or you will see stars) and concentrate on settling your body.
- Put both feet firmly on the ground so that they are well supported.
- Be aware of the chair under your legs and supporting your back.
- Allow yourself to sink into the chair.
- Push your shoulders down towards your feet, then stop pushing; if they jump back up towards your ears then repeat this.
- Remember your breathing – in and out through your mouth.
- Concentrate on the picture on your wall, scan the outline of shapes.
- Allow your eyes to close, gently and now let's settle your head.
- Allow it to roll very gently first to one side and then to the other.
- Now let it find a comfy spot for your head to settle.
- Open your mouth slightly and wiggle your bottom jaw. Swallow and rest your tongue on the bottom of your mouth. Now close your lips but *not* your teeth.
- Screw up your eyes and nose, then stop and allow them to relax.
- Allow the lines and frowns to go from your face, to smooth away and drain away your tension.
- Remember your breathing – in and out through your mouth.
- Think of your calming statements on your prompt card.
- Monitor your level of arousal – think of the thermometer.
- If you feel more calm and less angry and tense:

BE PLEASED WITH YOURSELF!
WELL DONE!!
THAT'S YOU TAKING CONTROL!

- Breathe in peace and relaxation.
- Breathe out the anger and tension.
- You can hear sounds around you, but that's OK – they are not talking to you – you don't have to answer – just concentrate on cooling down, coming down the scale.

- Eyes are gently closed.
- Now think again about what made you angry.
- Are you sure you got the facts right? – listened properly?
- Was it worth getting angry? Maybe not...?
- But if it is something you have to sort out and talk about, you will do it better if you are calm.
- So breathe in and out through your mouth.
- Remember, you can only do your best!

At the end of OTSAR

- Be aware of the sounds around you.
- Wiggle your fingers and toes.
- Open your eyes when you are ready.
- How do you feel? Where are you on the thermometer/scale?

An example of a customised version of step 5

Script – Use whenever you begin to get angry.

- *Stop Fred!*
- Breathe *out*.
- Take two deep breaths.
- Shoulders down and stretch your fingers.
- Steady breathing.
- Wiggle your bottom jaw and swallow.
- Take it easy, think it through.
- Breathe away the anger

SOME DO'S AND DON'TS OF RELAXATION AND BREATHING TECHNIQUES

Do:
- Remember relaxation is a skill that we have to learn (just like riding a bike!).
- Remember our bodies will not 'just relax' on cue just because we tell them to, just as our body does not 'get warm' on cue.
- Practise regularly.
- Find a quiet room with a bed, or a comfortable chair with a headrest.
- Later, try different positions, lying, sitting or standing.
- Undo any tight clothing such as a tie or belt, and remove spectacles.
- Once you can manage the techniques you can use them anywhere; you do not have to have a darkened room or a mat. (The lack of these things has been given as a reason for not practising the techniques!).
- Allow time to 'come to' slowly in a quiet room, otherwise all the good work can be undone very quickly.
- Use OTSAR anytime, anywhere.
- Remember that gradually the relaxation response is triggered more speedily.

Don't:
- Practise full relaxation too soon after a meal; leave it for about an hour between eating and relaxing.
- Try not to sleep when you are learning the techniques, you need to be awake to discriminate between tense and relaxed states.
- Sleeping does not prove that you are relaxed; we can all sleep when we are tense, hence those stiff necks in the morning!

THE ANGER THERMOMETER

The anger thermometer has proved to be useful when helping individuals to quantify their anger. It can be used as a teaching aid but also as a measurement tool for self-monitoring. Hence this follows the principles of cognitive behavioural work in a simplified form.

The wording used has evolved from user feedback. When individuals have their own set of labels that they refer to, the wording on the thermometer can be replaced with alternatives to suit the individual's preferences.

The thermometer can be used in a variety of ways:

A large version on thick card, say 50 x 70cm, used:

- as a teaching aid. A session could be devoted to creating this scale which then belongs to the group (adolescents seem to like this).
- with colour added to the thermometer, i.e. red at the top (near boiling) and cool blue at the bottom.

Small versions used as:

- a handout to increase awareness of anger arousal – useful for display on the bedroom door as a prompt!
- a self-monitoring sheet
- a blank handout which can be customised to include the individual's own wording or pictures
- as a picture in the individual's coping book.

ANGER THERMOMETER

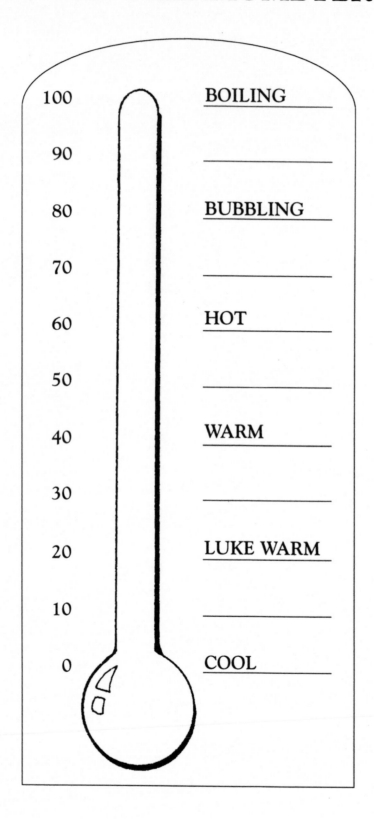

ANGER THERMOMETER

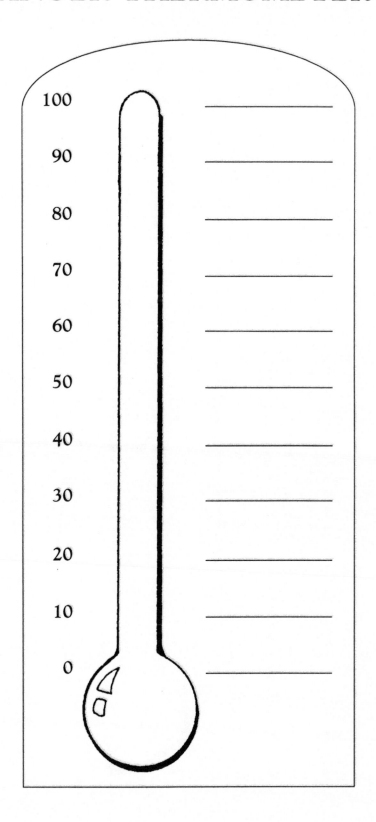

OUTLINE OF A PERSON

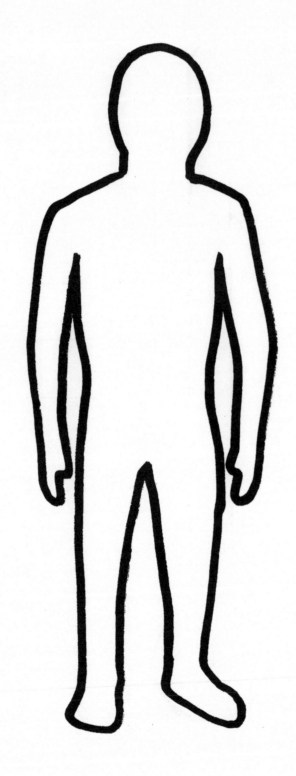

APPENDIX 2

THE COGNITIVE COMPONENT

GENERAL POSITIVE SELF-STATEMENTS

These are examples of positive self-statements. They can be used in Session 9 to contrast the 'wind-up' thoughts, and for self-instruction. This is a general list and is offered for those individuals whose discriminatory powers do not allow them to use the four stages of S.I.T. and for whom it is advisable to stick to a general statement that can be used at any time.

These self-statements should not be presented to the client so that they can just pick one; they are to inspire each individual who can then, with some help, formulate a list that is meaningful to them.

- Chill out!
- Calm down, take it easy.
- It's challenge time – relax.
- Don't take it personally.
- Breathe away the anger.
- Breathe deeply and slowly.
- It's time to stretch your jaw.
- Don't yell.
- Listen to what they have to say, give them a chance!
- Don't give them the satisfaction of seeing you angry.
- Don't get carried away.
- It won't kill me to do it.
- Ignore it/them.
- Don't get involved, it's not worth it.

- Don't worry, be happy!
- Did I listen properly and get the whole story?
- Just because they said *No*, it doesn't mean they don't care.
- Its not worth a fight, I can't always win.
- Some things even I can't solve.
- Who says we have to agree?
- It's not fair, but losing my temper will just make things worse
- Can't win 'em all!

POSITIVE SELF-STATEMENTS (four stages)

Examples of self-statements are given for each of the four stages in the sequence of anger arousal. A general list has also been given for those individuals whose discriminatory powers do not allow them to select which statement to use at which time.

STAGE 1 : PREPARING FOR PROVOCATION

- Breathe out and relax, you'll think more clearly.
- Remember what you are trying to sort out, stick to that.
- There won't be any need for an argument.
- Don't take what they say personally.
- Easy does it, try not to take it too seriously.
- This is going to upset me, but I can deal with it.
- Stop worrying. Worrying won't help anything.
- This is a challenge – relax!

STAGE 2 : DURING THE EVENT

- As long as I am cool I am in control.
- I don't have to prove myself.
- There's no point in getting cross/angry.
- It's a shame that he/she has to act like this; they must be very unhappy.
- I'm not going to let him/her get to me!
- Big slow breaths, stay focused, it will pass.

STAGE 3 : COPING WITH AROUSAL

- Time to take a big breath out.
- My anger is a warning sign, I need to move away and relax.
- This is a warning sign, I need to use my coping statements/card/etc.
- Shoulders down, and stretch out your fingers.
- Take it easy, don't get pushy.

STAGE 4 : LEAVING THE ANGER AND LOOKING BACK

- I did my best and handled it OK.
- That wasn't as bad as I had thought.
- I didn't win but I tried.
- That was a challenge now relax!
- Good, I did it! Next time I'll do even better!
- I didn't get angry!

ADDITIONAL EXERCISES FOR COGNITIVE WORK

USE OF RECORDED TV SOAPS OR DRAMAS

- Record a TV programme that involves interpersonal situations leading to disagreement.
- Allow the group to watch the recording. Then ask them to go to different areas of the room and write down, or orally report to a scribe, their understanding of the situation that they saw.
- This provides some understanding of how the individuals have appraised the situation. Discuss how some people:

  - are always 'getting the wrong end of the stick'
  - are on the look-out for annoyances (expecting trouble)
  - focus on what might be wrong about a situation – rather than what was OK (negative bias)
  - overgeneralise – if one thing goes wrong it seems to them that everything always goes wrong. Is there any evidence?
  - jump to conclusions before they know the facts (mind reading)
  - are quick to label others or themselves – 'he's a ...... fool', 'I'm a loser' instead of 'I made a mess of it today'. These character labels are 'wind-up' statements and do not encourage logical discussion.
  - blame others for their behaviour – this is a misattribution
  - use a lot of 'should' statements – this sets them up for anger and frustration. If they are aimed at themselves it can lead to resentment or even guilt (dictatorial thinking).

Should, *ought* and *must* are said to be illogical rules! In cognitive therapy they are thought of as one of the cognitive biases.

- All of these points can be used to provide a role-play of alternative endings to scenarios.

IT'S EASY TO LET YOUR THOUGHTS 'WIND YOU UP'

- At times we all get rapid thoughts rolling over in our heads.
- It is definitely worth being aware of this because it can lead us to draw the wrong conclusion and then get angry or worried unnecessarily.
- Wind-up thoughts seem to make so much sense at the time!
- As thoughts race, body arousal increases, and visa versa.
- Rolling thoughts *can* be interrupted, stopped and challenged.

An example of the problems of the rolling thoughts!

A client had lots of questions about his future community placement and benefits. He made frequent phone calls to his social worker and to his key worker. He was given answers to some of his questions but others were not readily available. On a bad day, when the client had spent a long time worrying about his unknown future, his thoughts became progressively more and more distorted, his arousal level increased as did his sense of injustice. He *was* going to find out what was going on! He phoned his social worker only to be told she was out (she had popped out of the office to buy a sandwich for lunch). The client's rolling thoughts were as follows:

She's not in again! she's never in when I want her, she doesn't care about me! might as well not have a social worker, I'll never get my future sorted out! nothing ever works out for me there's no point in staying on here, I'm going to discharge myself, I'm going to leave!

When looking at the straight facts of the scenario it seems that the client was going to discharge himself, all because his social worker has gone out to buy a sandwich! Does that make sense? **Discuss.**

TRYING TO SEE IT FROM THE OTHER PERSON'S POINT OF VIEW

Trying to see the situation from the other person's point of view, or role-taking, can be a useful exercise. As an angry incident has been reported in a session:

Try to get an accurate picture of the scenario.

- Set up a role-play to re-enact the scenario. Ask the angered person to take the part of him/herself, and reliable others to take other roles.
- After the role-play try to identify what the angry person was thinking as they were angry. These thoughts may be unrealistic or illogical but they were real at the time, so don't dismiss them; empathise instead.
- Now swap roles and repeat the role-play, with the angered person now playing the provocative one.
- Any feedback from the participants? Did the angered person gain any new understanding of the situation? Was there an alternative explanation for the person's behaviour? Discuss how things are not always what they first seem!
- If any labelling took place – *he's a failure!* look more carefully at the scenario and allow the client to explore whether they were basing that label on one mistake rather than a general comment. If so, a helpful reappraisal would be – *he got it wrong this time but he's not a failure as a person*.
- Try to challenge the individual's appraisal of the situation, if necessary.
- Use the opportunity to teach additional assertion and problem-solving skills.

WHAT ARE YOUR RULES FOR LIFE, AND DO THEY WORK?

We all have a set of rules for life. We adopt them as we are growing up and often they are very helpful, keep us out of trouble, and give us standards to live up to. However, some of these rules are so rigid they set us up to fail or get annoyed very easily, for example:

- I must always get things right.
- People who ask for help are whimps!

If someone follows these rules, or holds these assumptions, there is a danger that they would struggle to cope if they did need help. They would find it hard to ask for and, if they did, they might be unforgiving and angry with themselves!

Examples of other rules commonly held:

- If I apologise people will think I am backing down.

- Unless I'm on my guard all the time people will take advantage of me.
- Survival means hitting out before you get hit
- People should never be late!
- If I get angry, I'm a bad person.

Can you think of any more?

Now take one of these rules and try to work out the advantages and disadvantages of following them.

Example

Unless I'm on my guard all the time people will take advantage of me.

Advantages	Disadvantages
I might not get hurt so much.	I won't get close to anyone.
I will protect myself.	I won't trust anyone.
I won't get taken for granted.	I will think the worst of people,
I'll be looking out for them!	might then be provocative to them.
If people do, then it will	I will be lonely.
prove I'm right!	I will miss out on joining in things.

- Discuss if it actually works.
- Is it worth following, or is it a hindrance rather than a help?
- Is the rule realistic? – would other people try to follow it? – ask them.
- Can you think of a replacement rule that might be less rigid and therefore kinder to you because it will not set you up for anger and frustration?
- Now work through some of the other rules, or better still – think of your own! If the client is able to rate how much they believe in that life rule, then ask them to do so before the advantage/disadvantage exercise above. After the exercise repeat the belief rating and compare to the original, it may have reduced slightly. This is a way of shifting rigid rules or assumptions, but it is not a 'quick fix.'

BUBBLE PICTURE

HELPFUL CALMING THOUGHTS

'WIND UP' THOUGHTS

THE THINK – FEEL – DO SEQUENCE

THE THINK – FEEL – DO SEQUENCE

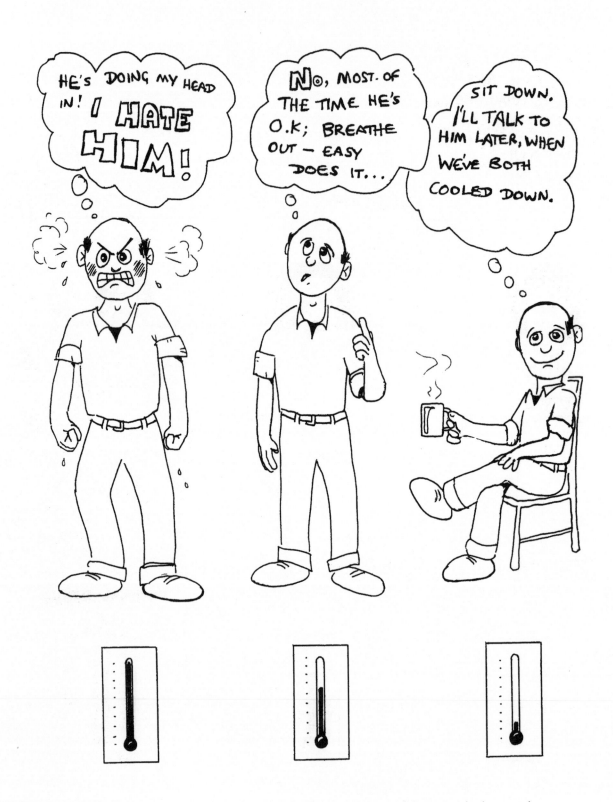

THE THINK – FEEL – DO SEQUENCE

THE THINK – FEEL – DO SEQUENCE

TAKE ANOTHER LOOK AT THE SITUATION THAT MADE YOU ANGRY

QUESTIONS TO ASK – if looking back at your diary or – rethinking the situation

1.   Was the initial reason for the anger justified?

- If so, think about this.
- Was there some other possible reason for the situation?
- Was there a misunderstanding?
- Did you pick up the wrong signs?
- Did you listen properly?
- Did you 'get the wrong end of the stick'?

2.   What were the unhelpful 'wind-up' thoughts?

3.   Did they fuel the anger?

Try to think of more constructive useful thoughts to use another time. Write some down on the blank column on your diary, e.g.

Instead of: *Why is she doing this to wind me up, it's always the same!*

Try: *Hey I'm not going to let her get to me! This is a hassle-free zone!*

STARTING TO FEEL ANGRY?

QUESTIONS TO ASK YOURSELF

- Have I listened properly?

- Have I got the facts right?

- Have I got the whole story?

- Should I ask for more explanation?

- Is it worth getting angry over?

CHALLENGING STATEMENTS AND QUESTIONS

- Maybe there's been a mistake.

- Have I explained myself clearly?

- I jumped in very quickly.

- Have I checked there is no other reason for this situation?

GETTING TO KNOW YOUR ANGRY THOUGHTS

FACTS:

1) They are automatic.

2) They are also called Negative Automatic Thoughts or NATS; *help – I've got NATS!!* But we all get them sometimes!

Tick which of these statements are about your angry thoughts

- They wind me up!

- They tend to lead to other similar thoughts – *then I'm on a roller!*

- They are personal to me

- They give me a strong message

- I really believe them!

- It is worth learning to spot them

- But they are hard to stop!

A space to write examples of your angry thoughts:

APPENDIX

3

THE BEHAVIOURAL COMPONENT

ASSERTION TRAINING

Learning to be assertive is an important part of anger management training. Like all of the other components, assertion training can be graded according to the individual's capability. First explain the meaning of *the assertive way* compared to that of being aggressive or passive see handout (page 164). Simple examples of the different behaviours may have to be given to help clarify the meanings of 'even more long words'!

Discuss the differing consequences of being assertive, aggressive or passive, for example:

*   Often the passive person feels angry a lot of the time.
*   The aggressive person may well lose friends.
*   The assertive person feels pleased with themselves for trying.
*   A poor self-esteem is associated with those who show either passive or aggressive behaviours.

So being assertive means saying clearly what you want, need and/or feel, whilst at the same time respecting the needs, wishes and feelings of others. It means putting your point and needs across to others:

*   saying clearly what you want or need
*   saying it in a way that means business
*   being able to say NO if you want to
*   saying what you want to say, and feeling better because you have 'said your piece', even if it doesn't change anything!

- having respect for others and yourself
- taking responsibility for your own actions and choices.

Examples of assertive statements

- *I feel annoyed because your loud music is bothering me.*
- *No, I just do not lend money to other people.*
- *Could you please put the cigarette out, it bothers me.*
- *Please can we talk about this and sort it out.*
- *I am sorry you are upset, can we make up?*

Being assertive is useful in situations such as:

- saying NO
- making requests
- giving criticism
- receiving criticism
- stating opinions
- explaining dissatisfaction
- leaving a situation when you want to – exit skills
- explaining that there has been a mistake
- dealing with 'wind-ups'
- defending yourself against criticism
- asking others to do their share
- refusing unwanted help
- refusing an unwanted invitation
- getting the wrong change
- explaining that your benefits are late
- apologising
- agreeing to disagree with others (e.g. over football teams)
- explaining you don't like the other person switching a video on when you are watching the TV
- your neighbour is playing very loud music!
- asking a favour
- when given an incorrect order in a restaurant or shop
- being short changed
- explaining a mistake at work
- interrupting and joining in with the crowd.

THE ASSERTIVE WAY

THE PROBLEM-SOLVING ROUTINE

Ask yourself the following questions:

1.   What am I concerned about?

2.   What do I want to happen?

3.   What can I do?

4.   What will happen if I...?

5.   What is my decision?

6.   Now do it!

7.   How did it work?

APPENDIX

4

DIARIES AND WORKSHEETS

DIARIES

There is unlimited scope for the design of diaries. A selection is provided in this appendix. They are listed in a progression, i.e. the early ones being more useful in the early part of the course.

The **WIND-UP SCALE** offers the opportunity to record a number (0-10, or 0-100) three times a day. This is so called for people who do not get angry but just get wound up! It needs to be accompanied by a measure, ie thermometer.

The **RECORD OF EMOTIONS** is used whilst learning to differentiate between emotions. There is space on the left of the page for simple drawings, cut-out pictures or colours that can be used as codes.

The **ANGER MANAGEMENT DIARIES** initially record information about 'the incident' and later involve information on arousal and the cognitive aspects. You will notice that the first version, which records the three components of anger – Thinking, Feeling and Doing – does not follow that sequence. Instead it is printed in the order – Feeling, Thought and Behaviour. This is because recording one's thoughts is usually considered more difficult than recording bodily feelings. If the client cannot fill in the first column he/she may well 'file it in the bin', thus reducing the likelihood of compliance with diaries. The second version of the cognitive-behavioural diary does follow the correct sequence, and the third version has a blank column in which to challenge thoughts.

DECIDE with the client where to keep the used diaries and who will have access to them. Diaries will contain information about others which, if read out of context, could be misconstrued or cause offence. Whatever is written in diaries is not fact, but it was real to the client at the time of writing it! Therefore, if other staff are going to access the diaries do remind them not to react defensively if they find damming information about themselves. Any such defensive reaction will in turn inhibit the client's future recording. Having said this, there is always the client who uses the diary as a way to shock!

WIND-UP SCALE

Name:

Week commencing:

	MON	TUE	WED	THU	FRI	SAT	SUN
MORNING							
AFTERNOON							
EVENING							

RECORD OF EMOTIONS

Name:

Week commencing:

	MON	TUE	WED	THU	FRI	SAT	SUN
MORNING							
AFTERNOON							
EVENING							

ANGER MANAGEMENT DIARY

Date	What made you angry?	How angry did you feel? 0–100	Anger thermometer
			BOILING — 100, 90 / BUBBLING — 80, 70 / HOT — 60, 50 / WARM — 40, 30 / LUKE WARM — 20, 10 / COOL — 0

ANGER MANAGEMENT DIARY

Write down when you feel annoyed **or** lose your temper. Try to do this as soon as possible afterwards.

DATE	SITUATION	FEELING: How my body changed	THOUGHT: What I was thinking to myself	BEHAVIOUR: What I did

DIARY

Try to use this diary each time you experience strong feelings and/or thoughts (these could be positive or negative)

DATE	SITUATION/ EVENT	AUTOMATIC THOUGHTS	ALTERNATIVE THOUGHTS ⊕	FEELING (Bodily changes)	BEHAVIOUR
Wed	In pub or shop. It was busy. Stood in queue to be served. A man was staring at me	Why is that guy staring at me? ⊖ Who the hell does he think he is? He deserves a 'bunch of fives'!	He doesn't know me – he's just interested in me or my clothes. He's not a threat	Breathing faster. Hot. Heart racing. Legs moving. Hands tense	Stared back and glared at him
Fri	Sitting in TV room with George who keeps on about my clothes and the mess around my chair	He is always picking on me. ⊖ Leave me alone!	He doesn't always – usually he is my friend. He often helps me	Gritting my teeth. Breath heavier. Stomach churns	Told him to 'p--- off!' Left the room and slammed the door!

Managing Anger, H O'Neill, © 1999. This may be copied for use with clients only.

DIARY

Try to use this diary each time you experience strong feelings and/or thoughts (these could be positive or negative)

DATE	SITUATION/ EVENT	AUTOMATIC THOUGHTS	ALTERNATIVE THOUGHTS	FEELING (Bodily changes)	BEHAVIOUR

ANGER MANAGEMENT DIARY

What triggered the problem? What was happening before?	What did you do? What happened next?	What happened after that? How did you feel?

ANGER MANAGEMENT

WAYS TO CALM YOUR

THOUGHTS	BODY	BEHAVIOUR
• Use self-instruction • Distraction • Count backwards • Imagery • Concentrate on something around you, e.g. the wallpaper, the clock-face, picture, etc. • Think of a funny picture • Traffic light sequence	• Arousal reduction • Breathe out first, then breathe in and out twice deeply • 10 slow breaths (count on fingers = interrupt anger sequence) • OTSAR • Use relaxation tape • Gentle rhythmical movement to music	• Move away separate from the others • Put hands by your side or in your pockets • Sit down in the chair, lean back and stretch those tense muscles • Change posture – stretch the body and 'break the tension' • Stretch out your arms, legs and fingers if sitting • Talk more slowly and quietly • Go for a walk • Listen to music • Swim • Exercise – remember to wind down at the end! • Get a cold drink • Find someone to talk to • Sing!

ANGER MANAGEMENT

WAYS TO CALM YOUR

THOUGHTS	BODY	BEHAVIOUR

THE TRAFFIC LIGHT ROUTINE

At the **first** sign of anger think of a set of traffic lights on red, so:

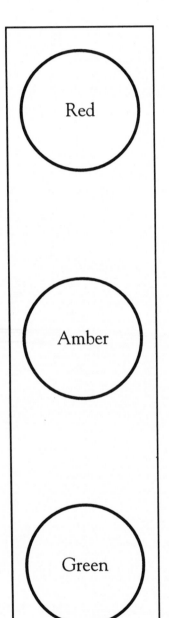

Shout out or imagine hearing the word
STOP!

GET READY – to calm down
Breathe out – blow away the anger
Stand still
Take two deep breaths

GO – move away
Take regular deep breaths
Use distraction techniques

THE TRAFFIC LIGHT ROUTINE

At the **first** sign of anger think of a set of traffic lights on red, so:

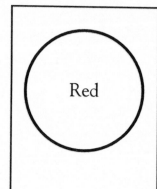

Danger
Stand still
Turn away

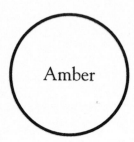

Think
Is it me?
Have I got the facts right?
Swallow
Breathe out
Nice thoughts

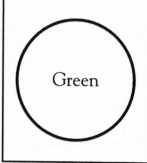

Go – (slowly)
Start again
Understand more
Know what you want
Speak slowly and clearly

THE TRAFFIC LIGHT ROUTINE

At the **first** sign of anger think of a set of traffic lights on red, so:

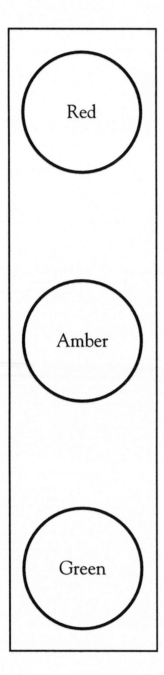

This sheet can be customised to the client's own wording

REFERENCES

If a reference is applicable to cognitive impairment, the author's name is in **bold**.

Alderman N, Knight C, Morgan C (1997) Use of a modified version of the Overt Aggression Scale in the measurement and assessment of aggressive behaviours following brain injury. Brain Injury 11: 503–23.

American Psychiatric Association (1994) Diagnostic and statistical manual of mental disorders IV. Washington, DC: APA.

Barratt E (1994) Impulsiveness and aggression. In Monahan J, Steadman H (Eds) Violence and Mental Disorder – Developments in risk assessment. Chicago: University of Chicago.

Bellack A, Hersen M (1984) Research Methods in Clinical Psychology. New York: Pergamon Press.

Benson B, Rice C, Miranti S (1986) Effects of anger management training with mentally retarded adults in group treatment. Journal of Consulting and Clinical Psychology 54: 728–9.

Benson H (1976 & 1985) The Relaxation Response, 6th edn. Glasgow: Collins.

Black L (1990) Treatment options for people with a mental handicap who are offenders. Issues in Criminology and Legal Psychology 16: 22–36.

Black L, Cullen C, Novaco RW (1997) Anger assessment for people with mild learning disabilities in secure settings. In Kroese B, Dagnan D, Loumidis K (Eds) Cognitive-Behaviour Therapy for People with Learning Disabilities. London: Routledge.

Black L, Novaco RW (1993) Treatment of anger with a developmentally handicapped man. In Wells R, Giannetti V (Eds). Casebook of the Brief Psychotherapies. London: Plenum Press.

Breakwell G (1989). Facing Physical Violence. London: BPS and Routledge.

Burns D (1990) The Feeling Good Handbook. New York: Plume.

Buss A, Perry M (1992) The aggression questionnaire. Journal of Personality and Social Psychology 63: 452–9.

Dagnan D, Chadwick P (1997) Cognitive-behaviour therapy for people with learning disabilities: assessment and intervention. In Kroese B, Dagnan D, Loumidis K (Eds) Cognitive-Behaviour Therapy for People with Learning Disabilities. London: Routledge.

Davis D, Boster L (1992) Cognitive-Behavioural-Expressive intervention with aggressive and resistant youths. Child Welfare LXXI (6).

Digiuseppe R, Tarfrate R, Eckhardt C (1994) Critical issues in the treatment of anger. Cognitive and Behavioural Practice 1: 111–32.

Digiuseppe R (1995) Developing the therapeutic alliance with angry clients. In Kassinove H (Ed) Anger Disorders: definition, diagnosis and treatment. Bristol: Taylor & Francis.

D'Zurilla T, Goldfried M (1971) Problem solving and behaviour modification. Journal of Abnormal Psychology 78: 107–26.

Eckhardt C, Deffenbacher J (1995) In Kassinove H (Ed) Anger Disorders: definition, diagnosis and treatment. Bristol: Taylor & Francis.

Feindler E (1991) Cognitive strategies in anger control interventions for children and adolescents. In Kendall PC (Ed) Child and Adolescent Therapy: cognitive-behavioral procedures. New York: Guilford Press.

Feindler E (1995) Ideal treatment package for children and adolescents with anger disorders. In Kassinove H (Ed) Anger Disorders: definition, diagnosis and treatment. Bristol: Taylor & Francis.

Feindler E, Ecton R (1986). Adolescent Anger Control. New York: Pergamon Press.

Goldstein A, Keller H (1987) Aggressive Behaviour: assessment and intervention. Oxford: Pergamon Press.

Jacobson E (1938) Progressive Relaxation. Chicago: University of Chicago Press (Midway reprint, 1974).

Howells K (1989) Anger management methods in relation to the prevention of violent behaviour. In Archer J, Browne K (Eds) Human Aggression: naturalistic approaches. London: Routledge.

Kellner M, Tutin J (1995) A school-based anger management program for developmentally and emotionally disabled high school students. Adolescence 30 (120): 813–25.

Kroese B, Dagnan D, Loumidis K (Eds) (1997) Cognitive-Behaviour Therapy for People with Learning Disabilities. London: Routledge.

Levey S, Howells K (1991) Anger and its management. Journal of Forensic Psychiatry 1: 305–27.

Liberman R, DeRisi W, Mueser K (1989) Social Skills Training for Psychiatric Patients. Boston: Allyn & Bacon.

Lindsay W, Baty F (1986a) Behavioural relaxation training. Mental Handicap 4: 160–2.

Lindsay W, Baty F (1986b) Abbreviated progressive relaxation. Mental Handicap 14: 121–6.

Lira F, Carne W, Masri A (1983) Treatment of anger and impulsivity in a brain damaged patient: a case study applying stress inoculation. Clinical Neuropsychology 5: 159–60.

McKay M, Rogers P, McKay J (1989) When Anger Hurts; quieting the storm within. Oakland, CA: New Harbinger Press.

Meichenbaum D (1975) A self-instructional approach to stress management: a proposal for stress inoculation . In Spielberger C, Sarason I (Eds) Stress and Anxiety, vol 2. New York: Wiley.

Meichenbaum D (1985) Stress Inoculation Training. New York: Pergamon Press.

Meichenbaum D, Goodman J (1971) Training impulsive children to talk to themselves: a means of developing self-control. Journal of Abnormal Psychology 77: 113–26.

Miller R, Rollnick S (1991) Motivational Interviewing. New York: Guilford Press.

Mitchell L (1977 and 1987) Simple Relaxation: the Mitchell method for easing tension, 2nd edn. London: John Murray.

Murphy G, Clare I (1991) MIETS: a service option for people with mild mental handicaps and challenging behaviours or psychiatric problems. 2 Assessment, treatment, and outcome for service users and service effectiveness. Mental Handicap Research 4: 180–206.

Novaco RW (1978) Anger and coping with stress. In Foreyt JP, Rathjen D (Eds) Cognitive Behaviour Therapy. Lexington, MA: Heath.

Novaco RW (1986) Anger as a clinical and social problem. In Blanchard R, Blanchard C (Eds) Advances in the Study of Aggression, vol 2. New York: Academic Press.

Novaco RW (1992) A contextual perspective of anger with relevance to blood pressure. In Johnson E, Gentry W, Julius S (Eds) Personality, Elevated Blood Pressure and Essential Hypertension. Washington: Hemisphere Publications.

Novaco RW (1993) Clinicians ought to view anger contextually. Behaviour Change 10: 208–18.

Novaco RW (1993–4) Stress Inoculation Treatment for Anger Control Therapist Procedures (1993–4 modifications). Available from Professor R Novaco, University of California, Irvine, CA92717, USA.

Novaco RW (1994a) Anger as a risk factor for violence among the mentally disordered. In Monahan J, Steadman H (Eds) Violence and Mental Disorder – developments in risk assessment. Chicago: University of Chicago Press.

Novaco RW (1994b) Clinical problems of anger and its assessment and regulation through a stress coping skills approach. In O'Donohue W, Krasner L (Eds) Handbook of Psychological Skill Training: clinical techniques and applications. Boston: Allyn & Bacon.

Novaco RW (1997) Remediating anger and aggression with violent offenders. Legal and Criminological Psychology 2: 77–88.

O'Callaghan M, Couvadelli B (1998) Use of self-instructional strategies with three neurologically impaired adults. Cognitive Therapy and Research 22(2): 91–107.

O'Neill H (1995) Anger: the assessment and treatment of problematic anger. British Journal of Occupational Therapy 58: 427–31 and 58: 469–72.

O'Neill H (1997) Relax, when I'm angry? You must be joking. Therapy Weekly, June 19.

Payne RA (1995) Relaxation Techniques: a practical handbook for the health care professional. London: Churchill Livingstone.

Pope S, Jones R (1996) The therapeutic effect of reactive self-monitoring on the reduction of inappropriate social and sterotypic behaviours. British Journal of Clinical Psychology 35: 585–94.

Poppen R (1989) Behavioural Relaxation Training and Assessment. Oxford: Pergamon Press.

Reed A, Clements J (1989) Assessing the understanding of emotional states in a population of adolescents and young adults with mental handicaps. In Kroese B, Dagnan D, Loumidis K (Eds) Cognitive-Behaviour Therapy for People with Learning Disabilities. London: Routledge.

Renwick S, Black L, Ramm M, Novaco R (1997) Anger treatment with forensic hospital patients. Legal and Criminal Psychology 2: 103–16.

Rosenberg M (1965) Society and the adolescent self-image. Princeton, New Jersey: Princeton University Press. This measure is available from NFER-NELSON Publishing Company Ltd, Darville House, 2 Oxford Road East, Windsor, Berkshire SL4 1DF.

Schilling D, Poppen R (1983) Behavioural relaxation training. Journal of Behaviour Therapy and Experimental Psychiatry 14: 99–107.

Schlichter K, Horan J (1981) Effects of stress inoculation on the anger and aggression management skills of institutionalized juvenile delinquents. Cognitive Therapy and Research 5: 359–65.

Spielberger C (1988) Manual for the State Trait Anger Expression Inventory. Odessa, FL: Psychological Assessment Resources.

Sunderland M, Engleheart P (1994) Draw on Your Emotions. Oxford: Winslow Press.

Tavris C (1989) The Misunderstood Emotion, 2nd edn. New York: Touchstone.

Uomoto M, Brockway A (1992) Anger management training for brain injured patients and their family members. Archives of Physical and Medical Rehabilitation 73: 674–9.

Wilcox D, Dowrick P (1992) Anger management with adolescents. Residential Treatment for Children and Youth 9(3): 29–39.

Williams H, Jones R (1997) Teaching cognitive self-regulation of independence and emotion control skills. In Kroese B, Dagnan D, Loumidis K (Eds) Cognitive-Behaviour Therapy for People with Learning Disabilities. London: Routledge.

Williams J (1990) Helping people to relax in over-stimulating environments. Mental Handicap 18: 160–2.

Wolpe J (1973) The Practice of Behaviour Therapy, 2nd edn. Oxford: Pergamon Press.

FURTHER READING

If a reference is applicable to cognitive impairment, the author's name is in **bold.**

Averill JR (1983) Studies on anger and aggression. American Psychologist 11: 1145–60

Crichton J (Ed) (1995) Psychiatric Patient Violence: risk and response. London: Duckworth.

Davis M, Eshelman E, McKay M (1995) The Relaxation and Stress Reduction Workbook. USA: New Harbinger Publications, Inc.

Deffenbacher J (1996) Cognitive behavioural approaches to anger reduction. In Dobson K, Craig K (Eds) Advances in Cognitive Behavioural Therapy. London: Sage.

Deffenbacher J, McNamara K, Stark R (1990) A comparison of cognitive-behavioural and process-orientated group counseling for general anger reduction. Journal of Counseling and Development 69: 167–72.

Dryden W (1990) Dealing With Anger Problems: rational-emotive therapeutic interventions. Florida: Professional Research Exchange Inc.

Grogan G (1991) Anger management: a perspective for occupational therapy. Occupational Therapy in Mental Health 11: 135–47 and 149–71.

Herst K, Gunn J (Eds) (1991) The Mentally Disordered Offender. London: Butterworth-Heinemann.

Holland S, Ward C (1998) Assertiveness. Oxford: Winslow Press.

Jacobson E (1976) You Must Relax. London: Unwin Paperbacks.

Kassinove H (1995) Anger Disorders: definition, diagnosis, and treatment. New York, Taylor & Francis.

Lidbetter S (1994) Cognitive approaches to anger management. Mental Health Nursing 14: 199–221.

Moon JR, Eisler RM (1983) Anger control: an experimental comparison of three behavioural treatments. Behaviour Therapy 14: 493–505.

Moore E, Adams E, ElsworthJ, Lewis J (1997) An anger management group for people with a learning disability. British Journal of Learning Disabilities 25: 53–7.

Novaco RW (1977) Stress inoculation: a cognitive therapy for anger and its application to a case of depression. Journal of Consulting and Clinical Psychology 45: 600–8.

Novaco RW (1979) The cognitive regulation of anger and stress. In Kendall P, Hollon S (Eds) Cognitive Behavioural Interventions. New York: Academic Press.

O'Neill H (1997) Anger management: is it a job for OTs? British Journal of Therapy and Rehabilitation 4: 352–3.

Reeder D (1991) Cognitive therapy of anger management: theoretical and practical considerations. Archives of Psychiatric Nursing 5: 147–50.

Reiss S, Rojahn J (1993) Joint occurrence of depression and aggression in children and adults with mental retardation. Journal of Intellectual Disability Research 37: 287–94.

Rossiter R, Hunnisett E, Pulsford M (1998) Anger management training and people with moderate to severe learning disabilities. British Journal of Learning Disabilities Vol. 26: 67–74.

Shepherd J (Ed) (1994)Violence in Health Care: a practical guide to coping with violence and caring for victims. London: Oxford University Press.

Stermac L (1987) Anger control treatment for forensic patients. Journal of Interpersonal Violence 1: 446–57.

Taylor E (1988) Anger Intervention. American Journal of Occupational Therapy 42: 147–54.

Tullock R (1991) Anger and violence. In Dryden W (Ed) Adult Clinical Problems: a cognitive behavioural approach. London: Routledge.

Participant Feedback

We would like you to tell us what you thought about the anger management course. This will help us when planning future courses.

Please could you comment on the following:

1. What did you like about the course?

2. Can you now recognise the 'warning' signs of anger?

3. Did you mind using a diary?

4. Can you remember any coping techniques?

5. Can you use any of them?

6. Do you feel the anger management course has helped you?

7. Give your reasons.

8. Is there anything that needs changing?

9. Any other comments?

Thank you for completing this form.